A gift

to

~~Community College of Allegheny County~~

from the collection of

Robert G. Colodny
Professor Emeritus
University of Pittsburgh

HD
6664
.G35

British Trade Unions

Elizabeth Gard

LONDON: Methuen & Co Ltd
NEW YORK: Roy Publishers Inc

First published 1970
by Methuen & Co Ltd
11 New Fetter Lane, London EC4
and Roy Publishers Inc, New York 10021

© 1970 Elizabeth Gard

All rights reserved. No part of this publication
may be reproduced, stored in a retrieval
system, or transmitted in any form or by any
means, electronic, mechanical, photo-
copying, recording or otherwise,
without the prior permission of the publisher.

Photoset by BAS Printers Ltd, Wallop, Hampshire
Printed in Great Britain
by Butler & Tanner Ltd
Frome, Somerset, and London

Methuen SBN 423 44070 5
Library of Congress Catalog Card No 77-113162

Contents

Introduction

1 Rich and poor
2 The journeymen's clubs
3 The Combination Acts
4 Outside the law 1799–1825
5 The Luddites
6 The repeal of the Combination Acts
7 The Industrial Revolution
8 Robert Owen and the Grand National
9 The Tolpuddle Martyrs
10 Lord Shaftesbury and the Factory Acts
11 The rise of the engineers
12 The New Model Unions
13 The Royal Commission of 1867
14 The TUC
15 Changing fortunes
16 The miners
17 Joseph Arch and the agricultural labourers
18 Socialism and the London Dock Strike
19 The birth of the Labour Party
20 From Taff Vale to the Osborne Judgement
21 The Labour unrest of 1910–14
22 The Triple Alliance
23 The First World War
24 Lloyd George and labour
25 The Slump and unemployment
26 The General Council and the First Labour Government
27 Red Friday
28 The General Strike
29 The General Council under Citrine and Bevin
30 The Second World War
31 The search for a wages policy
32 The need for reform

A select booklist
Index

Acknowledgements

Permission to reproduce illustrations is gratefully acknowledged to the Mansell Collection for numbers 1–7, 10 and 17; the Radio Times Hulton Picture Library for numbers 8, 11, 12, 14, 15, 16, 18, 19, 20, 21, 24, 25, 27, 28, 29 and 31–36; the Communist Party for number 30; the *Sun* for numbers 37, 38 and 39; and the Amalgamated Society of Woodworkers for number 9.

Introduction

The British trade union movement is the oldest in the world. Although trade unions as we know them today did not appear until the 1850s when Britain had become a highly-developed industrial country, their origins go at least another hundred years further back. Even before the beginning of the Industrial Revolution in the late eighteenth century, skilled workmen had learned how to combine together for mutal benefit. But the crucial years in the development of trade unionism were those between 1780 and 1840.

This period was marked by some of the most dramatic and rapid changes in British social and economic history. In 1780 the population was about $7\frac{1}{2}$ million; by 1840 it had leapt to 18 million, the fastest rise ever. In 1780 Manchester had about 50,000 inhabitants; by 1840 it had over 300,000. In 1780 the great majority of people lived in the country; by 1840 nearly half the population lived in towns. In 1780 the majority of men worked in agriculture; by 1840 three quarters worked in industry.

There were also subtle but important changes in the way people thought and spoke about social and economic matters. In 1780 the workers were often referred to as 'the lower orders' or 'the mob'. Words like 'working class', 'middle class', and 'industry', either did not exist or meant something different. 'Industry', for example, usually meant the opposite to idleness rather than the process of production. By 1840 all these words had acquired their modern meanings.

The development of industry in the modern sense changed the traditional relationship between rich and poor, between employers and employed. The poor and powerless, whether they worked in fields or factories, began to think of themselves and be thought of as 'the working class'. The spread of trade unions was a symptom of the increasing class-consciousness of the British people during the exciting but unhappy period of the Industrial Revolution.

1 Rich and poor

It is now almost impossible for us to imagine how wide the gulf was between rich and poor in the eighteenth century. Three quarters of the population lived in conditions of extreme poverty which would be considered intolerable today, while great landowners with annual incomes of £10,000–£50,000, a fortune in those days, were far richer than any modern British millionaires. Men like the Dukes of Newcastle and Bridgwater possessed more wealth and power than most European princes. They lived in magnificent style and were lavish spenders. The Fourth Duke of Devonshire, who succeeded to the title in 1755, spent £40,000 on alterations to Chatsworth House. In 1759 the Marquis of Rockingham spent £25,000 just on his stables and kennels.

Younger sons of younger sons, and extravagant gentlemen in distress, could usually scrounge a pension or salary from the Court. Non-existent jobs such as 'Keeper of the King's Tennis Court' or 'Taster of the King's Wine in Dublin' were worth several hundred pounds a year. One elderly baroness received a generous salary for being 'Sweeper of the Mall in the Park'. Modest squires of middling rank, bishops, bankers and large merchants with incomes of £2,000–£4,000, were all richer than most present-day managing directors of large companies.

Only a few highly-skilled craftsmen, such as the London goldsmiths and clock-makers, earned as much as £50 a year. Most craftsmen outside London earned between £30 and £40, enough to live in reasonable comfort and security. Town labourers, with an average of about £23 a year, and farm labourers with even less, lived on the brink of starvation. In 1780, the average wage of a farm labourer was about 8s 6d a week. (In some areas it was as low as 6s.) These wages were barely enough to provide a family with a scanty diet of bread, gruel and potatoes with an occasional stew or scrap of bacon. They left nothing for clothes, rent, fuel and other necessities, or for emergencies such as illness. Without the extra pennies women and children could earn at farm-work, domestic service or spinning and weaving, most rural families would have been destitute.

Extreme inequality was an accepted part of eighteenth-century life. Taxes were levied on food and other necessities rather than on incomes, so that they fell most heavily on the poor. The law was primarily designed to protect property, and the penalties for theft were appalling – a child could be hanged for stealing a handkerchief. Young gentlemen paid handsomely for commissions in the Army and Navy; labourers' sons could be herded into service by the press-gang. Wealthy noblemen spent huge sums on purchasing parliamentary seats and bribing the electors; the poor had no votes.

Few members of the upper classes thought there was anything unjust or morally wrong in this treatment of the poor. On the contrary, it was part of the natural order of things, deeply felt, and supported by centuries of religious and social practice. The following remarks are typical.

Everyone but an idiot knows that the lower classes must be kept poor or they will never be industrious.

The more lowly path of the poor has been alloted to them by the hand of God ... It is their part faithfully to discharge its duties and contentedly to discharge its inconveniences.

The first was made by Arthur Young, gentleman farmer and traveller, in his *Tours through England* (1760–80); the second by William Wilberforce, a devout Christian and the leader of the crusade against Negro slavery.

The rich at least recognised a duty to prevent the poor from starving. Under the Poor Laws they paid rates to the parish authorities which were responsible for tramps and beggars, widows and orphans, the old and the sick. But the poor were expected to be grateful for any bounties they received and not to treat them as their right. It was their duty to 'know their place'.

2 The journeymen's clubs

It was not until the first stages of the Industrial Revolution that this idea of a society in which everyone 'knew their place' began to crumble. One of the first signs of change was the formation of journeymen's clubs.

Apart from a few large and important industries like woollen cloth, iron, and ship-building, most manufacturing in the eighteenth century was done in small workshops by a master craftsman, his assistants, usually called journeymen, apprentices and labourers. Until about 1750 there was little feeling that masters and journeymen had different or clashing interests. After all, most masters had once been journeymen, and many journeymen would one day become masters. Rates of pay and the supervision of apprenticeships were fixed by custom and administered by the magistrates.

Towards the end of the century, relations between masters and journeymen grew increasingly bitter. There were two main reasons for this. Firstly, the rapidly rising population and the war against France (1793–1815) brought a steady increase in the demand for manufactured goods. In order to raise production and make bigger profits, manufacturers needed larger workshops, more capital and more and cheaper labour. Frequently they sidestepped the laws on apprentices and broke customary wage-agreements. Usually the magistrates did little or nothing to stop them, much to the indignation of the journeymen. Secondly, as industries grew larger the journeymen found

1 *Pictorial heading to the list of resolutions drawn up at a meeting of London hat-makers, 1820. The Feltmakers had one of the earliest of the journeymen's clubs.*

it more difficult to save enough money to set up on their own.

So they drew apart from the masters into Trade Clubs and Friendly Societies with elaborate names like The Original Society of Painters and Glaziers and The London Sailmakers' Burial Society. Each member paid a subscription into a fund which was spent on books, newspapers, social activities and benefits covering sickness, unemployment and funeral expenses.

Although the clubs were small and local, any member could visit his particular trade's club in another town and get information about jobs. This arrangement was known as 'tramping'. A man 'on tramp' usually went to the public house where journeymen from his trade regularly met. (Inn-signs such as The Bricklayers' Arms and The Carpenters' Arms are often clues to the early history of the trade union movement.)

In spite of the bar-room setting, club meetings were usually sober and serious. Many members were self-educated men able to read and write and talk intelligently on industry and politics. The leaders were often devout Methodists who imposed strict rules against drunkenness, swearing and fighting. The Glassmakers sternly banned 'persons who are infamous, quarrelsome or disorderly'.

This included all 'ignorant and impudent labourers', whom the craftsmen regarded as a threat both to their social life and their craft standards and wages. Their clubs provided a double protection against the unskilled workers below them and the masters above.

3 The Combination Acts

Towards the end of the century the journeymen's clubs began to organise resistance against employers who broke traditional agreements on wages and apprentices, and to write indignant petitions to Parliament. But the government sided with the employers, who were sending equally indignant petitions about the way their journeymen were 'combining' against them. In each case a special Act was passed against the combination in question. Finally the government decided to pass comprehensive Acts to suppress 'this general disease in society'.

Under the *Combination Acts* of 1799 and 1800, anyone joining a combination for the purpose of opposing his employer could be sentenced to three months in prison or two months' hard labour. These penalties were fairly mild in comparison with those already imposed under common laws against strikes, violent disobedience, machine-breaking, and other offences. In practice workmen could hardly act in combination without falling foul of the law. The Combination Acts were significant for their definition of all combinations as illegal, and their provisions for quick trials, rather than for their severity.

The passing of the Combination Acts, together with the gradual shedding by the government of its traditional responsibilities for the regulation of industry, marked a victory for the principle known as *laissez-faire*. This was the idea that industry should be left to run itself without state interference.

Everything was supposed to find its right market price according to the balance of supply and demand. This applied to both labour and raw materials. So to the manufacturer there was not much difference between a man's labour and a bale of cotton. He tried to buy both as cheaply as possible in order to undercut his rivals.

In practice, *laissez-faire* was completely one-sided. The employers were free to haggle and bargain, but the workers were not. They had to take whatever price was offered for their labour. The employers were able to get together and fix wages for their trade or district, but the workers were not. They were left, without government protection, without even the right to protect themselves, to 'find their market price'.

The government had another reason for passing the Combination Acts. The bloody events of the 1789 French Revolution had struck terror into the hearts of the British ruling classes and made them view with alarm any sign of rebellion at home. Their fears multiplied after 1793 when England went to war with France.

They had reason to be fearful. Many people in Britain opposed the war, and openly sympathised with the French revolutionaries' desire for 'Liberty, Equality and Fraternity'. The Prime Minister, William Pitt, remarked, 'My head would be off in six months were I to resign.' In 1795 the harvest failed and there were bread-riots all over the country. King George III was hissed and pelted with

2 *Cartoon by Gillray of George III being attacked by the mob in 1795. Pitt is the driver.*

stones as he drove in his state coach to open Parliament. In 1797 the sailors of the Nore Fleet mutinied, and in 1798 a rebellion broke out in Ireland.

In reply the government passed a whole series of repressive Acts against political meetings, radical clubs and newspapers, and the swearing of 'unlawful oaths'. Although the journeymen's clubs were not primarily political, many of their members also belonged to radical groups. So the Combination Acts were designed to thwart the political as well as the industrial ambitions of the artisans.

4 Outside the law 1799-1825

During the course of the war against Napoleon political opposition subsided. But in spite of the Combination Acts, journeymen's clubs became more numerous and bolder. This was partly because the laws were clumsily enforced. As there was no proper police force, it was difficult to catch offenders, particularly as many combinations disguised themselves as innocent Friendly Societies with no interest in trade matters. And it was partly because many small masters were prepared to tolerate combinations and even to co-operate with them.

Sometimes the journeymen tried to browbeat the employers. In 1801 for example, a South Shields shipyard owner received an anonymous note which said:

You Mr Bulmer, if you do not give the carpenters a guinea a week, as sure as Hell is Hot O, before winter is done you will be Shot O.

The intrepid Mr Bulmer threatened to use the Combination Acts against his men and eventually received a public apology, but other employers were frightened into surrender by these strong-arm methods.

But the fear of the law made combining workmen tread warily. They had always to be on guard against government spies posing as members of their societies. Trade unionism became a sort of underground movement protected by secrecy and ready to meet any emergency. The tailors, for instance, were organised on almost military lines, with a pre-arranged second line of command ready to take over if their leaders were arrested. They called themselves The Knights of the Needle and their combination was so strong that masters had to consult them before employing a new man. The tailors and other similarly well organised groups of artisans managed to increase their wages.

In some respects persecution only strengthened the trade unions, and drew the working classes closer together. Shut out from politics, and with a shared experience of hardship, hunger and insecurity, they sought comradeship in their unions. They began to address each other as 'brother' and 'loving shopmate'. Many trade union traditions took root during these illegal years, including their own special vocabulary:

black-list a list of union trouble-makers circulated among employers

scab a man who betrays his mates

blackleg a non-union man who works during a strike. (This word was invented by the miners who could always tell that a man had been down a pit during the strike by his coal-blackened legs.)

The very words *trade union* began for the first time to be widely used.

5 The Luddites

The sterner prosecution laws against rebellious workmen together with the acceptance by the government of *laissez-faire* gave manufacturers more power over their work-people then ever before. In some trades, particularly textiles, they ruthlessly squeezed more and more work out of them for less and less money.

Their most pitiful victims were the hand-loom weavers, cotton-spinners and stocking-knitters. These were usually piece-workers — people who were paid for each finished article rather than by the hour or week. In the 1790s they had been prosperous and independent, earning about 30s. a week. During the early nineteenth century their pay had been relentlessly cut until by 1835 it was down to 5s for a working week of up to 90 hours. (Imagine what it would be like nowadays to drop from £30 a week to £5.)

In 1814 the Nottingham stockingers sent a 'Humble Address' to the Lord Lieutenant asking for a 'Reasonable Advancement':

Think what our feelings must be when our little ones cling around our knees for bread, which we are unable to give them! Though we have substituted meal and water, or potatoes and salt for that more wholesome food an Englishman's table used to abound with, we have repeatedly retired after a hard day's labour, and been under the necessity of putting our children supperless to bed, to stifle their cries of hunger.

The Lord Lieutenant merely told them to 'bear up manfully'. But the piece-workers could not help comparing their situation with that of prosperous artisans in other trades, and concluding that the only answer lay in combination. However, because they were in such a weak position, their unions rarely lasted long, and tended to be wild and violent. Government spies were constantly reporting stories of midnight meetings on the moors, of record books buried underground, and of fearsome oaths sworn at pistol point.

The most alarming outbreaks of violence on the fringes of the trade-union movement started when hundreds of Nottingham stockingers, enraged by the introduction of a new type of knitting-frame, joined a secret society which was led by a mysterious character called General Ned Ludd. According to legend, his headquarters were in Sherwood Forest. Nobody knows to this day who he was or whether he really existed at all. But the stockingers certainly believed in him.

In 1881, gangs of masked 'Luddites' broke into workshops at night and smashed the frames of any employers who had reduced or used unapprenticed labour. During the next few years there were similar attacks on textile machinery in Yorkshire and Lancashire. On several occasions, there were pitched battles between the raiders and the owner's men, in which a number of people were killed. Eventually, the ring-leaders were captured, and by 1814 Luddism had petered out. 25 men, 1 woman and a youth of 16 were hanged, and hundreds of others were transported in convict ships to Australia.

6 The repeal of the Combination Acts

The Combination Acts were eventually repealed in 1826. This important victory for the unions was due almost entirely to the efforts of Francis Place, a self-made master-tailor. Place was born in the London slums and had been apprenticed at the age of fourteen to a maker of gentlemen's breeches. Five years later he was involved in an unsuccessful strike and out of a job. Unable to get work because of his reputation as a trouble-maker, he spent two years of desperate poverty during which he somehow managed to educate himself in politics and economics by browsing in bookshops.

In 1795 he was elected secretary of the newly-formed Breeches-Makers' Society, and soon won his members a pay-increase. His own fortunes improved too, and he bought a shop in Charing Cross Road. Before long he was a prosperous man and was able to devote himself to his campaign for the repeal of the Combination Acts. Most men in his position would have sat back and enjoyed their hard-earned prosperity, but Place never forgot that he had once been a struggling journeyman.

The remarkable thing about Place was that he no longer approved of combinations, because he had been converted to the fashionable *laissez-faire* theories. He wanted the laws repealed simply because they had proved useless and dangerous. Not only were there more combinations than ever, but there were more strikes, more bullying, more violence. Place believed that this was

3 *Francis Place*

because the workers felt they had to stand together against the law, and that once the Acts were abolished the combinations would quietly fade away.

Although this line of reasoning turned out to be completely wrong, it was probably the only one that could convince Parliament. Though not himself a member, Place had a few allies in the House of Commons, and through them he converted the new Prime Minister, Sir Robert Peel, to his point of view.

Immediately after the repeal, hundreds of new combinations were formed and there was a rush of strikes and wage demands, due rather to a period of good trade and rising prices than to the repeal. The government's reaction was to pass another law stiffening the penalties against 'molesting, intimidating or obstructing' either employers or fellow-workmen. So, although the right to combine was recognised and combinations as such were no longer criminal, workmen continued to be punished for much the same offences as before.

13

7 The Industrial Revolution

The words 'Industrial Revolution' make us think of huge factories springing up almost overnight, belching smoke over what was once a 'green and pleasant land'. But the change was neither so sudden nor so complete. Even by the 1830s comparatively few people worked in factories. Most skilled artisans still worked in small workshops and most labourers still did mainly casual work, on roads or building sites, or in the docks.

When people spoke in the early nineteenth century of an Industrial Revolution, they were usually thinking of the great new textile factories of Yorkshire and Lancashire with their steam-driven machinery. The growing industrial cities, like Manchester, Bolton and Leeds, became almost a world apart, inhabited by two new tribes; the wealthy capitalist factory-owners, and the urban industrial 'masses'. Factory life on such a scale as this was new, and the experience of the factory hands were quite unlike those of previous generations.

At first most of them came into the cities from nearby districts. Some had been farm labourers, but the majority were hand weavers and spinners unable any longer to make a living from piece-work. Only a few were given skilled jobs in the factories. Whatever their former work and standard of life, nearly all of them worked as unskilled machine operatives. The manufacturers wanted cheap plentiful labour, people who could easily be trained for simple, repetitive work, and who were naturally obedient and docile. Women and children were ideal for their purposes. Sometimes a man could only get a job if he promised to bring his wife and children into the factory with him.

One of the main sources of cheap labour, especially in the early stages, were the workhouses. The Poor Law Overseers were only too pleased to supply large numbers of beggar boys or whole pauper families. In Leeds and Manchester they even set up labour markets, where suitable families could be inspected and hired.

This motley collection of workers did not settle quickly or easily into factory life. They were used to hard work and a continual struggle against poverty, but they were not used to the harsh factory discipline: hours of work dictated by the factory bell, fines for arriving late or leaving early, and lists of regulations on the wall:

Any spinner found with his window open ... fine 1s.
Any spinner found dirty at his work ... fine 1s.
Any spinner found washing himself ... fine 1s.
Any spinner heard whistling ... fine 1s.

These were just a few of the rules in force at a cotton mill in Tydesley, Lancashire, where spinners worked a 14-hour day in a stifling atmosphere of 27°C (80°F). They must have seemed intolerable to people who had been used to doing their work in their own time, and to eating, talking, singing or whistling

4 *Factory children, by Francis Trollope, 1839*

whenever they pleased.

Perhaps the greatest evil of the factory system was the destruction of normal family life. When the whole family worked at home, the mother spared at least a little time for cleaning, cooking and taking care of her babies. But factory wives came home only to sleep. They hardly saw their children at home, except to pull them out of bed at 4 am and pack them off to work.

The widespread practice of employing women and children in preference to men meant that many fathers were more or less dependent on the earnings of their families. In some mills men were sacked at the age of twenty-one when they became eligible for the higher adult wage. Some of them found odd labouring jobs, but others became completely demoralised and turned to drink and crime.

The towns in which they lived were ugly and unhealthy. There were no parks and trees, no proper water supplies, no street-cleaning or rubbish collection. Diseases and epidemics swept through the mean streets of crowded little houses. In Manchester just over half the children died under the age of five. One Manchester doctor described the mill-workers as 'a new degenerate race — human beings stunted, enfeebled and depraved.' A crippled spinner wrote:

A factory labourer can be very easily known as he is going along the streets; some of his joints are sure to be wrong. Either the knees are in, the ankles swelled, one shoulder lower than the other, or he is round-shouldered, pigeon-chested or in some other way deformed.

These were the inevitable scars of grinding toil under the most appalling conditions. Thousands died of asthma and lung complaints after inhaling air thick with fumes, steam, dust and bits of flying waste. Others were crippled by continual stooping. Children developed rickets from being kept on their feet all day. In some mills they or their parents were fined if they sat down for a rest, which encouraged mothers and fathers to bully their own children. If they fainted or fell asleep, they were often slapped and kicked, or plunged head down into a bucket of water.

All the horrifying details of the sufferings of

factory workers in the early nineteenth century were recorded in the Reports of several Parliamentary Enquiries. Although it was not until the 1840s that the government took effective action to protect the workers, the Reports did at least awaken the consciences of a few MPs. Most of them, however, remained indifferent, even to such stories as this:

Joseph Hebergram, aged seventeen, had worked in worsted spinning factories at Huddersfield since he was seven:

When I had worked about a year, a weakness fell into my knees and ankles; it continued and it has got worse and worse. In the morning I could scarcely walk, and my brother and sister used out of kindness to take me under each arm, and run with me, a good mile, to the mill, and my legs dragged on the ground in consequence of the pain; I could not walk. If we were five minutes late the overseer would take a strap and beat us till we were black and blue.

The employers of these miserable people justified themselves on both practical and moral grounds. They insisted that they were forced to keep their factories working day and night because they started with only a small borrowed capital, and had to make quick profits in order to survive. Manufacturing was a fiercely competitive business: for every man who made a fortune, there were hundreds who failed. It was in everyone's interests that they should not fail. After all, they were public benefactors who brought wealth to the country and gave employment to thousands. Ignorant people should be grateful for the chance to work eighty hours a week: it was good for their characters; it saved them from the worst of all sins — idleness.

Many of them sincerely believed in these chilling arguments. A few were actually sadistic. But the majority were merely callous and hypocritical, indifferent to the misery that surrounded them. They allowed their overseers to bully and brutalise — sometimes even encouraged them. They held such a low view of their employees that they became almost completely indifferent to them as human beings.

Most of them were self-made men who regarded their own success as proof of the virtue of hard work. They felt that any man worth his salt would rise to the top, and those who did not must be lazy and inferior. Unlike the small workshop masters, many of whom were equally hard taskmasters, the newly-rich factory-owners neither lived nor worked alongside their employees. More and more, they drew themselves apart from the ordinary townspeople. As early as 1818 a Manchester cotton spinner complained:

They are literally petty monarchs ... who in the pride of their hearts think themselves the Lords of the Universe.

8 Robert Owen and the Grand National

5 *Robert Owen*

There were a few manufacturers who took a kindly interest in their work people, and paid decent wages for reasonable hours – and still made a profit. The most remarkable of these reforming employers was Robert Owen, the owner of the huge New Lanark cotton mills in Scotland. He was a highly-successful businessman and made a fortune. But this did not satisfy him. He wanted the workers to share in the new wealth and abundance of the machine age.

He started by building for his employees a model town with fine houses, shops and schools, which became famous throughout the country. Then he turned to revolutionary schemes for co-operative communities where men would live as brothers and share equally all the fruits of their labours. He was the first real *Socialist* leader and thinker. Naturally he was considered by his own class to be a dangerous crank, but to the working class he became something of a hero.

Owen's ideas were followed enthusiastically by a new generation of ambitious young trade unionists, the most important of whom was an inspiring and eloquent Irish cotton-spinner called John Doherty. Even while the Combination Acts were still in force, Doherty had made several attempts to organise the Lancashire spinners into effective unions. But the employers had always been too strong for them and all their strikes or 'turn-outs' had been disastrous failures.

In 1830 Doherty formed the Grand Union of Operative Spinners and soon had a large membership. But he had grander ideas; he wanted one huge national union drawn from workers of all trades, who would all stand together in time of need. As a start he formed the National Association for the Protection of Labour, which was centred in Lancashire but soon spread as far as Wales and Birmingham. It all sounded most impressive, and there was a general air of excitement and optimism amongst its members. But its ambitions outstripped its funds and organisation. It failed to win its first strike and quickly collapsed. The Grand Spinners Union died with it.

Nothing daunted, Doherty embarked upon an even grander scheme. In 1834 he started the Grand National Consolidated Trade Union. By this time, in spite of the failure of earlier ventures, the idea of general unionism was gaining ground. The response to the Grand National was overwhelming. In less than a year, it had over a million members — more than the whole parliamentary electorate! Some of the old craft societies joined, but the majority of members were factory-hands, often women, few of whom belonged to other unions.

Fired by this success, the leaders of the Grand National declared that they would overturn capitalist society by staging a series of strikes, after which the workers would step in and take over the factories.

The government was greatly alarmed by this wild talk and decided to crush the Grand National. It chose as its victims the defenceless farm-labourers.

9 The Tolpuddle Martyrs

The plight of the rural poor in the 1830s was just as desperate as that of the urban workers. The textile factories had robbed them of extra earnings from spinning and weaving. Agriculture, which had enjoyed a period of prosperity during the wars against France, was in a state of depression. A rise in the birthrate had led to over-population in the villages and a surplus of labour. Wages fell to such a low level that in some villages three quarters of the population were dependent on parish charity. Squires and farmers could be just as ruthless as manufacturers. The landowners' tradition of kindly paternalism was fading. They became obsessed with the protection of their property against the starving and hostile poor. Woods and fields were laced with murderous booby traps and the penalties for breaking the Game Laws were cruelly increased.

In 1830 the failure of the harvest brought widespread starvation, and there was a wave of rioting and rick-burning throughout the southern counties. The labourers were unorganised and unarmed, and their revolt was savagely suppressed. Nine men and boys were executed, and 847 people, including several women, either transported or imprisoned with hard labour.

Then in 1834, in the Dorset village of Tolpuddle, a group of men lead by two brothers, George and John Loveless, went to a meeting addressed by delegates from the Grand National. Afterwards they formed a local Friendly Society of Agricultural Labourers. It was all done with great ceremony and seriousness. Members took an oath of secrecy under the watchful eye of a painted figure of Death. They were quiet law-abiding men – several of them Methodist preachers. They would never have taken such a step had not the local farmers just reduced their wages to 7s. a week, 3s. less than in neighbouring counties.

Before they had so much as asked for a rise, the local magistrate had the six leaders arrested. They were tried under an Act passed during the 1797 naval mutiny which forbade the swearing of 'unlawful oaths', and given the maximum sentence – seven years transportation. In his defence, George Loveless, said, 'We are uniting to preserve ourselves, our wives and our children from utter degradation and starvation. We had injured no man's reputation, character, person or property.' But, as the judge remarked, they were not being sentenced for any particular crime but 'as an example to the working class of this country'.

The trial of the Tolpuddle Martyrs caused an outcry. It seemed as if the repeal of the Combination Acts had meant nothing. Robert Owen was so shocked by the trial that he joined the Grand National and organised a huge demonstration of protest in London. Four years later, after ceaseless agitation from a small group of unionists, the government relented and the Tolpuddle labourers were brought home. By that time however, the Grand National had already collapsed.

6 &**7** *A hostile view of working-class unrest from Maclean's* Life of a Labourer, *1830. (Above) A trades' union committee. (Below) Farm labourers wrecking threshing machines.*

followers dreams and ambitions that could not be fulfilled. He made them believe that social revolution and universal happiness were within their grasp. But all his schemes failed for lack of money and organisation. The Grand National could not keep pace with all the strikes that it encouraged, and its money soon ran out. Many of its members never paid their subscriptions, and in the end the treasurer ran off with the kitty, an all too frequent custom in the early days of trade unions.

10 Lord Shaftesbury and the Factory Acts

The failure of the Grand National demonstrated how helpless the factory workers were to resist the harsh conditions imposed upon them by their employers. But fortunately there were a few sympathetic men in Parliament who tried to awaken the conscience of the rich to the miseries of the poor. In particular there was Lord Shaftesbury, one of the noblest and most selfless figures of the Victorian age.

Shaftesbury was a deeply religious man whose passionate concern for human suffering set him apart from the majority of his class. He was no democrat, and thought that trade unionists were selfish men seeking to better themselves at the expense of their fellow-workers. He believed that the welfare of the poor was the responsibility of the ruling classes, a responsibility which they had shockingly neglected.

In 1842 he put before Parliament the Report of his Children's Employment Commission for Mines. It revealed that in most mining areas women and children were employed in heavy work underground. The Commission reported their appearance as 'indescribably disgusting and unnatural ... chained, belted, harnessed like dogs in a go-cart, saturated with wet and more than half naked, they crawl upon their hands and feet dragging their heavy loads behind them'. The report contained stories of terrified children crouching in the dark for anything up to twelve hours a day; of children starting underground work at the age of five; even of babies born down the pits.

The report shocked Parliament (especially its reference to the 'half-naked' pit-girls) and Shaftesbury's Act was passed. It forbade the employment underground of women and all children except boys over ten, and provided for regular inspections of mines.

Shaftesbury then turned his attention to factories. Earlier Factory Acts, banning the employment of children under nine and limiting the hours of older children, had proved ineffective. The factory inspectors had no real powers and employers found

21

innumerable ways of hoodwinking them. Sometimes they even hid their under-age children in the lavatories during inspections.

In spite of protests from employers that any limit on the hours of women and children would upset the factory routine and lead to shorter hours for men as well, Parliament was eventually converted to Shaftesbury's point of view. In 1847 a Factory Act was passed which set a limit of ten hours a day for women and 'young persons' and appointed extra inspectors to enforce it.

The *Mines Act* and the *Ten Hours Act* were signs of a more humane attitude towards the working classes. The government began to accept at least some responsibility for industry and other aspects of urban life. In 1847 and 1848 the first modest measures were taken to improve Public Health and the supply of gas and water. Some of the worst evils of the early 'get rich quick' stage of the Industrial Revolution were beginning to fade. Factory wages crept up and factory families became acclimatised to city life. But there was a limit to the improvements that could be expected from employers whose main object after all was to make money, or from a Parliament for which the workers were unable to vote. Their best hope of advancement was through their own efforts, particularly through their trade unions.

11 The rise of the engineers

In 1842 there were about 100,000 trade unionists in Britain, only a tiny fraction of the whole working population. There were no effective unions for unskilled labourers, and even amongst skilled workers union or 'society' men were in a minority of about ten to one. The strongest unions were centred on traditional and prosperous trades like coach-building and stonemasonry, and in the rising trades of the machine age like ship-building, engineering and iron-moulding, where skilled men were in great demand and could earn good money.

Yet even the most prosperous artisan could never feel really secure. A month's sickness, an accident at work, the shut-down of a factory, could drive him to the workhouse. In all the big cities there were usually a number of artisans temporarily out of work, pitiful in their fallen pride. A trade union was a good defence in bad times. It gave a man a sense of dignity and offered the companionship of a club. Also, at a time when there was no help from the state in the form of sickness or unemployment benefit, the unions' friendly benefits provided an insurance policy. To many members these things were more important than the pursuit of higher wages.

Throughout the 1840s the number of small local engineering unions steadily increased. In 1851 the largest of these, the Manchester Old Mechanics, persuaded the others to combine or amalgamate with it into one big union. So the Amalgamated Society of Engineers was formed, with William Allan of the Old Mechanics as its first General Secretary. The ASE was the ancestor of the presented Amalgamated Engineering Union and the father of modern trade unionism. 1851 was an appropriate birth-date, for it was in that year that Britain was recognised as the 'Workshop of the World' at the Great Exhibition in Hyde Park, which was dominated by the engineering industry.

The novelty of the ASE lay not so much in its size as in its organisation. It was the first national union to be centrally controlled and the first to have a full-time paid secretary. Although local branches kept a certain independence, every important question was referred to the London office. The Executive Council made the decisions, but only after local branches had been consulted — an arrangement which was both orderly and democratic. The ASE had a weekly income of over £500. Members paid a subscription of 1s. a week, a lot even for men earning 30s. But benefits were generous: 10s. a week unemployment, sick pay for fourteen weeks and 5s. for a further period; retirement pensions; injury grants of up to £100; and £10 funeral benefit. Any money left over went into the Reserve Fund for emergencies.

The engineering craftsmen were men of sober and thrifty habits. They paid their subscriptions regularly and did not drink at meetings. (Many of the old craft societies had spent up to a third of their income on beer!) Allan was equally sober and thrifty in matters of union policy. He wanted to build up the funds by avoiding costly disputes, and only gave official union support to strikes which the Executive considered absolutely necessary.

His main concern was to gain security for the ASE members by sharing out the available work as fairly as possible. The unions opposed compulsory overtime and the use of cheap untrained labour because these practices threatened the jobs of its members and debased the standards of their trade. The ASE believed that the qualified engineer was just as well entitled to protect his professional standards as a doctor or a lawyer, and that union membership should be the hallmark of a good workman.

But the engineering employers disliked all unions, however moderate and respectable. They insisted on their right to strike individual man-to-man bargains with their employees, and resented any form of collective bargaining, although they felt no such qualms about forming associations among themselves to resist the workers' demands.

In November 1851, the ASE informed the employers at Oldham that its members would stop working overtime after December 31st. The Employers' Association saw this as an

8 *Inside an iron foundry*

opportunity to crush the union. On January 10th, without any warning, the Lancashire and London employers shut their works. It was a 'lock-out' — a strike in reverse. The workers were told that they would get their jobs back only if they signed 'the Document' — a written promise to renounce the union.

The ASE suggested arbitration (judgement by independent outsiders) but the employers refused. The ASE then offered to drop their overtime ban if the employers withdrew the Document. Again they refused; they wanted total victory. The men hung on, supported by contributions from fellow-members, other unions and outside sympathisers, which amounted to £20,000. But by April the ASE funds were down to £700 and the locked-out men could fight no longer. They returned to work on the old terms and signed the hated Document.

The ASE had been defeated but not destroyed, for the employers soon discovered that the Document was useless. Men just signed it and stayed in the union; because it had been forced on them they did not consider it binding.

In the long run the lock-out strengthened the ASE. It revealed the remarkable determination and solidarity of the engineers. The employers' lawyer admitted:

They were exceedingly true to each other. They did not give in until they were entirely starved; I do not think the masters would hold out until they were ruined.

The loyalty of his members gave Allan a firm base on which to rebuild the Amalgamated Society of Engineers. By 1866, with a membership of 33,000 and a reserve fund of £140,000, it was the strongest and richest union that had ever existed.

24

12 The New Model Unions

During the 1860s a number of other craft unions followed the engineers' example. The bricklayers, the stonemasons, the iron-moulders and several other groups amalgamated into larger unions and modelled their organisations on the ASE. The strongest of these New Model Unions was the Amalgamated Society of Carpenters and Joiners, which soon rivalled the ASE itself in size and importance.

The General Secretary of the ASCJ, Robert Applegarth, was the most impressive trade-union leader of the time. He was a Yorkshireman, the son of a sailor, and a skilled cabinet-maker by trade. He was a man of immense energy; years later, when he was famous enough to be included in *Who's Who*, he listed his hobbies as 'Work, more work, and more again.' He was a good talker and very tough in spite of his small size. This is how he describes his first negotiation with an employer:

You're from the Union?

Yes.

Well, I shall cut you short.

Pray don't, I'm only five foot two and that's quite short enough.

In spite of, or perhaps because of, his bravado, he got what he wanted.

Applegarth's moderation, his disapproval of rough manners and drunkenness, his interest in education and self-improvement, above all his passionate concern for the dignity of working men, all earned him the respect not only of his fellow-unionists, but also of his opponents. He and others like him gave the trade-union movement a character of solid good sense and respectability. They were a new breed of trade-union 'civil servants', these new model general secretaries, who had exchanged a life of manual work for a life of accounting, letter-writing and speech-making. They no longer looked like workmen, but dressed in high silk hats and sober suits fastened with gold watch-chains.

In 1860 this group formed the London Trades Council, which soon became the headquarters of the trade-union movement. The LTC's main duty was 'to watch over the general interests of labour, political and social, both in and out of Parliament'. By 'labour' they meant the small section of the working classes to which their members belonged – the better-off skilled artisans. The interests of this 'labour aristocracy' were different from and often quite opposed to the interests of the unskilled labourers.

A 'labour aristocrat' was a man who regularly earned between 28s. and 40s. a week, enough to enable him to save something for his retirement. He was a steady worker who took pride in his craft. Although he worked long hours, he often found time to teach himself to read and write and to keep himself informed on political and industrial matters. He usually lived in a well-built, comfortable house outside the slum areas, and had little contact with the poorer, rougher, labouring man except at work. In some trades such as building and carpentry he might have several labourers under his charge. Often, under a system known as sub-contracting, he had to hire and pay his own labourers, so that he was himself an employer on a modest scale.

Most labour aristocrats were independent, self-employed men, and were not tied to any one firm. Usually they contracted to do a specific job for which they were paid either a set sum each day or week, or a piece-rate. Secure employment and regularity of earnings were just as important to them as the amount they earned. They scorned happy-go lucky types like the gas-stokers and railway navvies, who might earn 30s. one week and nothing the next. They believed in thrift and temperance; casual work and irregular hours did not encourage these virtues.

The New Model Unions exactly reflected the sober and conservative character of their members. In the words of the LTC official history, they only wanted to 'remould society so as to give the honest, sober, thrifty and industrious working man a better chance in life', by pressing for certain specific reforms in industry and politics. They did not threaten the established order: on the contrary they intended to become part of it.

The LTC's first goal was to win the vote for the more prosperous artisans; the second was to get a few trade unionists into Parliament. The first aim was partially achieved in 1867 when the Second Reform Act was passed. Nearly a million skilled workers in the towns were given the vote, and the size of the electorate was doubled. The second was not achieved for another seven years.

The main concern of the New Model Unions was to keep wages up by limiting the supply of skilled men. They realised that the price of labour depended mainly on the balance of supply and demand, and that the reason why unskilled labourers were so badly paid and so badly treated was that they were too plentiful. So they kept a careful check on the number of apprentices entering their trades, and whenever work was scarce, they encouraged their members to emigrate to America, Canada or Australia. They also tried to keep the labour supply evenly distributed throughout Britain by circulating information about jobs in different areas and by helping members with their travelling expenses.

Their attitude to disputes with employers was cautious and moderate. They believed that more could be achieved by bargaining than by bullying. Applegarth's advice was 'Never surrender the right to strike, but be careful how you use a double-edged weapon.' Like other general secretaries, he did not want to waste precious union funds on hopeless ventures and he knew how few strikes were successful. The LTC followed a realistic if sometimes unpopular policy of withholding financial support from any strike that it considered futile.

9 *A typical New Model Union membership card*

This was not because the New Model leaders were cowardly or complacent, but because they wanted to convince the employers that they were reasonable men. They knew that most employers distrusted unions of any kind and would do all in their power to destroy them. They knew also that this distrust was shared by most upper- and middle-class people. Even Charles Dickens, who did so much through his novels to expose the injustices and cruelties of mid-Victorian England, disapproved of trade unions. In *Hard Times* he describes the union as a selfish tyranny and its leaders as smooth-tongued schemers. The hero of the book, Stephen Blackpool, is an honest workman who refuses to join the union in the face of persecution by his workmates.

The LTC realised that its most important task was to make trade unionism recognised as respectable and necessary. Union members were urged to spend more time in the library and less in the pub. Meanwhile leaders like Applegarth explained the unions' case in newspaper articles, lectures and letters to MPs. This campaign was fairly successful. Gradually the trade unions gained a number of useful middle-class allies: politicians, lawyers, university professors, even a handful of businessmen.

13 The Royal Commission of 1867

In October 1866 a can of gunpowder was thrown down the chimney of the home of a Sheffield saw-grinder. No one was hurt, but the house was blown to pieces. The intended victim was a non-union man, and the suspected culprits were members of the Saw-grinders' Union. The public outcry against this desperate and futile crime was not only against the guilty union but against trade unionism in general.

The following year the unions had another setback. The Bradford branch treasurer of the Boilermakers' Society embezzled £24 of union funds. When the Society took him to court, the judge ruled that trade union funds were not entitled to legal protection because the money might sometimes be used for purposes that were illegal under Common Law. This case (*Hornby v. Close*) revealed the muddled state of the laws relating to trade unions, particularly those which had been passed at the time of the repeal of the Combination Acts in 1825. In theory it was virtually impossible for a union to organise a strike without breaking these laws. In practice their application had been so haphazard that the unions never knew where they stood.

In 1867 the government appointed a Royal Commission to examine the position of trade unions. The LTC welcomed it and appointed a committee of five known as the Junta to handle the unions' case. Applegarth, who was made chief union witness, said:

If a searching investigation leads to the discovery of an ulcer in our system, however small it may be, let the knife go to the very core.

At first it seemed as if the Commission would turn out to be hostile. Inquiries into the Sheffield gunpowder incident revealed that this was just one amongst many similar acts of violence committed by the Grinders' Unions. They had beaten up blacklegs, bullied non-union men and stolen their tools, and had murdered an unpopular employer. But Applegarth convinced the Commission that the grinders were not altogether to blame because working conditions were so bad that they only lived for an average of twenty-eight years; moreover that kind of aggressive local union was dying out, and the Commission should concentrate instead on the large Amalgamated Societies.

For two years the Commissioners heard evidence from all the interested parties. On the whole they were impressed by the organisation and finances of the New Model Unions, particularly by their benefit schemes. But they sympathised with employers' complaints about 'restrictive practices' relating to apprentices, overtime and piece-work. Also they were concerned about the position of non-union men.

This was a particularly difficult question. If the unions should be free to seek advantages for their members through collective bargaining and strikes, should not non-union men be equally free to refuse to join in? The Commission thought that they should be.

10 *A Sheffield workshop, 1866. Saw grinders at work.*

But in practice unions always tried to persuade as many workers as possible to join them so as to make their collective action more effective. During a strike, unions usually posted men as 'pickets' to persuade blacklegs not to take over the strikers' jobs. But if a blackleg refused to be persuaded, the pickets might threaten to beat him up; they might even carry out the threat.

A minority of Commissioners argued that without the right of picketing, unions would be unable to organise strikes and would be completely powerless. They also recommended that there should be no special laws against unions which did not equally apply to ordinary citizens. But the majority thought that picketing should be forbidden and that all the existing laws limiting union activities should remain in force.

In 1871 the government passed two new labour laws based on the majority report of the Royal Commission. The Trade Union Act granted full legality to the unions and protection for their funds. But the Criminal Law Amendment Act prohibited any form of picketing. The first Act disappointed all those employers who had hoped that the government would ban trade unions altogether. The second was a severe blow even to the most moderate union leaders. It was like being told, 'You can play football so long as you don't kick the ball.'

14 The TUC

During the 1860s there had been several large conferences in the provinces to discuss specific questions such as lock-outs and anti union laws. Then in 1868 the Manchester Trades Council organised a Trade Union Congress which was attended by delegates representing over 100,000 unionists. It was decided that the Congress should meet annually in different cities and should be a forum for discussion and debate.

At first the LTC cold-shouldered the TUC because the latter seemed to challenge its leadership of the movement. Also many of the unions represented in the TUC opposed the policies of the Amalgamated Societies, and criticised the LTC for being smug, timid, and tight-fisted in its attitude to strikes. But because of the obvious threat presented to the whole movement by the anti-picketing law, the two rival factions were reconciled at the third TUC which was held in London in 1871. 57 delegates attended, representing 300,000 members of 49 different unions.

The most important measure taken by the 1871 Congress was the setting up of a Parliamentary Committee, which was to be a sort of trade-union Cabinet. Its two main tasks were to organise a campaign against all anti-union laws, and to work towards the elections of friendly MPs to the next Parliament. It was remarkably successful in both.

Disraeli's Conservative government of 1874 was surprisingly sympathetic to the working classes. In 1875 the Criminal Law Amendment Act was repealed and replaced by a new Act which stated that a strike was not a crime and peaceful picketing would be allowed. Then came the repeal of the unpopular Master and Servant Act, which applied to cases of breach of contract. Under this Act, which fell particularly heavily on the miners, any worker who failed to finish a job could be imprisoned, whereas an employer who sacked a man before the end of his contract was only liable to pay the wages due. The new Employers and Workmen Act was much fairer. The very changes in words from 'Master' to 'Employer' and 'Servant' to 'Workmen' was a sign of a more modern and tolerant attitude. Between 1874 and 1880 the government passed several more reforming laws, on public health, housing and primary education, all of which helped the working classes, as well as a Factory Act limiting the hours of textile workers to fifty-seven a week.

These welcome reforms were partly due to the eloquence of the first two working-class men to enter Parliament — Thomas Burt and Alexander MacDonald. They were both miners: Burt was Secretary of the Northumberland Miners' Union, and MacDonald President of the National Miners' Union. They had achieved success through stamina and self-discipline. Like so many miners' leaders of their time, they were both devout chapel-goers and stern teetotallers. Although they had worked long hours down the mines since early boyhood, they were both well-educated men. From the age of eight, MacDonald had walked four miles each evening after work to the village school. By the time he was twenty-five he had saved enough money to go to Glasgow University, though he continued to work as a miner during his vacations.

Both Burt and MacDonald joined the Liberal Party in Parliament and were known as Lib/Labs. By 1886 there were ten Lib/Lab members, including the Secretary of the TUC Parliamentary Committee, Henry Broadhurst. He must have taken his seat with special pride, for as a young man he had once worked with hammer and chisel on the rebuilding of the House of Commons. His career was a fitting symbol of the political advance of the working class.

15 Changing fortunes

Between 1871 and 1875 total membership of trade unions doubled, reaching nearly $1\frac{1}{4}$ million. Several important new unions were started, and the movement began to spread to semi-skilled and unskilled workers. The main reason for this spurt forward was the trade boom. All through its history the trade-union movement has been strongest during periods of full employment and high wages. This is because employers are more prepared to make concessions to their workers when business is good. Also, in the nineteenth century, higher wages meant that more workers could afford to pay union subscriptions.

The leaders of the strong, skilled unions were optimistic about the future. Their confidence in capitalist industry seemed justified. By 1871 Britain's trade exceeded that of France, Germany and Italy combined. By 1873 exports were four times as great as in 1850. Profits reached record level and many large fortunes were made. The policy of most unions was to keep on good terms with the bosses and pick up as many crumbs as possible from the rich men's tables. The cotton and shipbuilding unions even invested union funds in shares in their own industries.

The 1870s also saw the first signs of regular consultation between the two sides of industry. Several unions, notably the iron-workers and miners, accepted a method of wage-fixing known as the 'sliding scale', whereby wages were tied to the selling price of their products. They thought at the time that they would gain more by this than by fixing standard minimum wage-rates. But they were soon proved tragically wrong.

From 1876 onwards both industry and agriculture fell into decline and did not recover until 1888. The reasons for the Great Depression were complex; the results

11 *Unemployment during the Great Depression, as illustrated in* Punch

12 *'Bloody Sunday', November 1887. Violence during a mass-meeting of the unemployed in Hyde Park, London.*

were stark and simple. Unemployment rose and wages fell. Casual and unskilled workers were hardest hit, but many skilled men, including trade unionists, either lost their jobs or suffered severe wage-cuts. As a result there were fierce strikes in one industry after another, but all were defeated.

The effect of the slump on the unions was drastic. Membership shrank miserably, until by 1884 it was less than half the 1874 figure of 1,200,000. Union finances were badly strained by the demand for unemployment benefits and strike pay. (In 1878 the ASE paid out more to its members than in all the previous twenty-six years of its existence.)

The scarcity of jobs lead to 'demarcation' disputes — quarrels between different unions as to who had the right to certain jobs. The leadership of the TUC, embodied in the portly person of Henry Broadhurst, did little or nothing about this particularly knotty problem.

Perhaps the most unfortunate result of the slump was the complete collapse of several of the newer unions, including the National Miners Union and the National Agricultural Union. For while they lasted, they had raised the spirits of thousands of the most oppressed workers in the land.

16 The miners

The miners lived almost like a race apart in grimy villages of one-roomed houses. Most of them were sons, grandsons and great-grandsons of miners; they had known no other way of life for generations. Because of their isolation, and because of the appalling dangers of their work, they were intensely loyal to each other. This bond had been tested and strengthened in many bitter struggles against their tyrannical employers.

The mine-owners were not simply businessmen; they were mostly great land-owners for whom the discovery of coal had been an unexpected bonus to the family fortune. They owned not only the mines and coal, but the villages and the shops — on one occasion the Marquess of Londonderry even claimed to own the miners. They would stop at nothing to break a strike or destroy a union. They imported blacklegs, often from the Continent; they evicted the strikers from their cottages and forbade the shopkeepers to sell them food on credit. Yet although the

mine-owners won strike after strike and smashed union after union, they could never kill the *spirit* of union.

The basic strength of mining unionism lay in small local unions, at pit, county or district level. These were the foundations upon which larger national federations were built. Unlike unions in other trades, they were not confined to skilled men but were open to all grades.

In the 1860s two important national unions were formed: MacDonald's National Miners Union, and the Amalgamated Association of Miners, based in Lancashire and Wales. By 1873 they each claimed over 100,000 members.

MacDonald believed that the best way to improve the miners' conditions was through Parliament. First, he wanted the government to improve the safety of the pits, which had been shockingly neglected by the owners. Bad ventilation, rotten timber-props and inflammable gases caused hundreds of deaths each year.

Second, he wanted a fairer system of payment. The miner was paid according to the amount of coal he sent up to the surface. Whenever his tub was not absolutely full, or contained more than a certain amount of coal-dust or stone, a fine was deducted from his wages. It was quite common for a man to lose his whole week's pay in fines. The miners wanted to elect their own 'checkweighers' to see fair play. In 1860 Parliament gave them this right, but the owners usually got rid of the checkweighmen by sacking them. It was not until 1887 that further laws abolished this abuse.

MacDonald's great triumph was to persuade the government to pass a Coal Mines Regulation Act in 1872, which provided for stricter safety measures and regular inspections. By 1880 both of the large national unions had collapsed in the Great Depression, but this Act remained as a monument to their efforts.

17 Joseph Arch and the agricultural labourers

Between 1850 and 1873 landowners and farmers enjoyed a period of unprecedented prosperity. But the farm-labourers' standard of living had improved little since the trial of the Tolpuddle Martyrs in 1834. In Dorset their average wage was still only 10s. in 1870. They still lived mainly on bread and potatoes and kettle-broth (a pathetic substitute for tea, made from burnt bread soaked in boiling water). When their working lives were over, thousands had no alternative but to creep to the workhouse to die.

The miseries of the rural poor are vividly described in the *Autobiography* of Joseph Arch, a Warwickshire labourer who in the 1870s became one of the finest leaders in the history of the trade-union movement. For years Arch despaired of rousing his fellow-labourers to resistance; they were 'voiceless, voteless and hopeless'. 'Years of poverty had ground the spirit of independence right out of them … the spirit of servitude was bred in their very bones.' But, he said, 'in season and out I was on at them, dropping the seeds of manly discontent', in the hope that one day they would form a union – 'a thumping big union'.

Then one night in February 1872, at Wellesbourne in Warwickshire, Arch held his first meeting. Under a large chestnut tree hung with lanterns, he stood on a pig-stool and 'spoke straight and strong for union' to two thousand local labourers. This was the start of the Warwickshire Agricultural Labourers Union which immediately organised a strike for 16s. a week. Most Warwickshire men then earned about 14s., but even this was above the national average of 12s.

13 *Joseph Arch holds a lamplight meeting at Wellesbourne, Warwickshire, in 1872*

14 *A group of agricultural labourers, c 1880*

The news of the strike spread like wildfire, and labourers all over the country began to organise.

Sometimes we gathered under a tree, sometimes in a field ... We met by sunlight and moonlight and starlight and lanternlight.

In May 1872 a National Agricultural Labourers' Union was formed. Within a year it had more than 100,000 members. Its aims were 16s. a week, a $9\frac{1}{2}$-hour day, and the vote for farmworkers.

At first the landowners, farmers and parsons who thought of the labourers as ignorant and docile creatures, ridiculed the union. The Bishop of Gloucester suggested that a ducking in the village pond would bring the agitators to their sense. But, as Joseph Arch put it:

'The bigwigs soon found out that I was a labouring man they had to reckon with; that if they tried to tread on my toes I trod back with hobnailed boots.

For two years he and his lieutenants travelled round organising strikes, and they were remarkably successful both in increasing wages and reducing working hours.

But in 1874 the farmers joined forces for a widespread lock-out, followed by the sacking and eviction of union men. It was cruelly timed. The harvest had just been gathered and winter was approaching. After a few months on the brink of starvation, most unionists gave up. And then from 1876 onwards there was a terrible agricultural depression. Prices tumbled and wages fell to their old levels. The National Union dwindled to a shadow of its former self, until by 1881 only 15,000 members were left.

Yet the memory of those stirring days remained, and in 1885, when the farm-labourers at last received the vote, Joseph Arch was elected to Parliament by the men he had so bravely led.

18 Socialism and the London Dock Strike

During the Great Depression the established trade unions became increasingly defensive. They resisted wage-reduction by any means short of strike action, and tried to protect the interests of skilled workers against competition from less-skilled men or labour-saving machinery. In politics they remained respectably Liberal.

Some of their members felt scornful and angry about the timidity of the official leadership. During the late 1880s the ideas of Karl Marx, the great Socialist thinker and writer, founder of Communism, gained a hold upon a number of impatient young trade unionists. Encouraged and instructed by a small group of middle-class Socialists, they campaigned against any form of co-operation with capitalists, either in industry or in politics. Their long-term aims were equal shares for all in the wealth of the country, the take-over of government by the workers, and public ownership of industry. Their short-term aims were trade unions for all grades, and an eight-hour day for every worker.

The most energetic of these Socialist trade unionists were Tom Mann and John Burns, who were both rebellious members of the ASE. In 1886 Mann wrote:

How long, how long will you be content with the present half-hearted policy of your unions? ... the true Unionist policy of aggression seem entirely lost sight of.

The first sign of aggression came from an entirely unexpected quarter – from the match-girls of the Bryant and May factory in

15 *Members of the Matchmakers' Union at Bryant & May's, 1888*

London's East End. The match-girls worked extremely long hours and were miserably paid. Many of them suffered from a disgusting disease called 'phossy-jaw', caused by touching sulphur, which made their teeth fall out and rotted their jaw bones. They would probably have continued to suffer in silence but for the publicity given to their plight by

Annie Besant, an ardent middle-class Socialist. Her campaign aroused so much public indignation that the employers were shamed into improving the match-girls' pay and conditions.

The following year the London gas-workers formed a union – the Gasworkers and General Labourers' Union – and demanded an eight-hour day. The employers gave in at once rather than risk a strike. The gas-workers' victory, said Tom Mann, *'put older and larger Trade Unions to shame'*. It had been won by men who were considered by respectable unionists as rough, uneducated louts incapable and unworthy of organisation.

Yet they had found a fine leader from among their own kind – Will Thorne. His parents had both been labourers in the Birmingham brick-fields. When he was seven, his father was killed in a bar-room fight; and he had been sent to work in a rope-works, where he earned 2s. 6d. for a twelve-hour day. As a young man he joined a travelling gang of road navvies. It was a brutal life. The navvies earned good money but spent most of it on drink and gambling. Their favourite pastime was watching dog-fights, or fights between dogs and rats in a pit, and betting on the result.

Thorne's experiences as a navvy convinced him that the labourers needed more than better wages. They needed more free time to spend with their families, and they needed education. He set the lead by taking a pledge never to drink and by learning to read and write. When he became a gas-worker he devoted himself to forming a union which would give the labourers a pride in them-selves, and secure a reduction in working hours. In both he was successful.

By 1946 when he died, he had been a trade-union General Secretary for forty-five years, Mayor of West Ham and a Member of Parliament. Both in his career and his personal life Thorne proved that a rough labourer could be worthy of respect.

The news of the gas-workers' victory spread like wild-fire and set the London docks ablaze. In August 1889 the dockers came out on strike – a strike which showed that even the dregs of labour (and the casual dockers were considered to be the dregs) could stand up for themselves, given the right sort of leadership. The dockers' leader Ben Tillet was an even more unlikely hero than Will Thorne. A wizened little man who had been a circus-boy, pit-boy, deckhand and low-grade docker, Tillet had always been treated with amused contempt by foremen and employers. He was nothing more than a 'dock rat'. Yet he had great ability and ambition. He was a friend of Mann and Burns, and at that stage he too was a fierce Socialist. In his autobiography he wrote:

In my dreams of economic warfare I saw how the Thames might and could be made idle ... and a thousand millions of financial power brought to a standstill.

In 1899 he was only the secretary of a small, weak union, but when his members

16 *Dockers queuing for a day's work, c 1889*

became involved in a minor dispute, he seized the opportunity of turning it into a huge strike. Mann and Burns came to his aid, and the skilled stevedores' union promised its support. But the dockers themselves were hardly good material for a union. Tillet himself admitted that *'these starved and dispirited men were not easy to fill with a spirit of revolt'.*

They were completely demoralised by the casual nature of employment in the docks, which was not by the week or even the day, but by the hour.

To obtain employment, Tillet wrote, *we are driven into a shed Iron-barred from end to end outside of which a contractor or foreman walks up and down with the air of a dealer in a cattle market, picking and choosing from a crowd of men who in their eagerness to obtain employment trample each other under foot, and where like beasts they fight for the chance of a day's work.*

He reckoned that there were about a hundred men for every job available, and those jobs went to the strongest. Old men sometimes dyed their hair in a pathetic attempt to disguise their age. Some weeks a docker might get only four or five hours' work. This made it impossible for him to buy enough food to give him the strength needed for hard manual labour. Quite often he was so weak and hungry that even when he got two or three hours' work he would pay himself off after the first hour and spend his first 5d. on a meal, perhaps his first meal for several days.

Such were the men in Tillet's army. As to the high command, Tillet admitted, 'we had only 7s. 6d. in the treasury, and all the union machinery there was, I carried, so to speak under my hat'. Yet the response to the strike was overwhelming. Within three days 10,000 men had stopped work and the Port of London was closed for the first time in a hundred years. Tom Mann organised the pickets with military discipline. John Burns, his black beard bristling and his eyes blazing, conspicuous in a white straw hat, led processions of dockers daily through the City of London to attract sympathy and support. With a figure of Neptune at their head and a brass band playing *Rule Britannia*, the dockers marched through the streets with their wives and children, brandishing pikes on which they stuck the 'docker's dinner' — old fish heads and dry bread.

Their obvious poverty touched the consciences and the pockets of the watching citizens, Altogether £20,000 of strike relief was collected from well-wishers. Even so, after three weeks some of the marchers began to collapse from hunger. But for an unexpected gift of £30,000 from Australian unions, the strike would certainly have been beaten.

After five weeks the employers were persuaded to give in by Cardinal Manning, who acted as mediator. The dockers got sixpence an hour — 'the dockers' tanner' — eightpence for overtime, and the promise of more regular employment. But most important of all they had gained a union, the Dock Wharf Riverside and General Labourers' Union, which by the end of November had 30,000 members.

The gas-workers and dockers received no encouragement from the official TUC leadership. According to Tillet, they were regarded as 'illegitimate offspring' by the well-established craft unions. But this indifference did not stop other groups of unskilled and semi-skilled workers from following their lead in forming general unions. Seamen, railway labourers, farm-workers, even waiters and laundresses, joined the movement. And in 1889 a new Miners Federation of Great Britain was formed, more militant than previous large miners' organisations.

These new unions were open to all grades, had low subscriptions and offered no benefits except strike-pay. They saw themselves not as insurance clubs but as 'fighting unions'. In the words of the Yorkshire miners they were fighting for *'Eight hours work, eight hours pay, eight hours sleep and eight bob a day*!

During the 1890s there were bitter debates at the TUC between the 'new' unionists and the 'old' Lib/Lab unionists. At the 1890 TUC John Burns remarked upon the difference in appearance of the rival groups.

The 'old' unionists ... looked like respectable city gentlemen; wore very good coats, large watch chains and high hats ... Amongst the new delegates not a single one wore a tall hat. They looked workmen, they were workmen.

After 1895, however, the gulf between the 'old' and 'new' unions narrowed. This was partly because the 'new' unions grew more moderate and respectable, but mainly because of changes in the composition and character of the 'old' unions. The division between skilled and unskilled labour was being blurred by the increasing mechanisation of industry. Craft unions like the ASE had to open their membership to lower grades. As they lost their old exclusiveness, the leaders became more sympathetic to the needs of unskilled and semi-skilled workers, and more militant. Their traditional faith in moderation was undermined by the continuing hostility of the employers to all types of union.

The new fighting spirit attracted many new members. Between 1888 and 1890, total membership of trade unions rose from 750,000 to a record total of nearly 2 million. Yet the workers' share in the growing wealth of the country hardly increased at all. Even cautious leaders began to lose patience and look for new policies. Robert Knight, the Boilermakers' leader, told the TUC:

The workman may be ignorant of the sciences and the arts ... but he is not blind ... He sees a large and growing class enjoying inherited abundance. He sees miles of costly residences each occupied by fewer people than are crowded into single rooms of the tenement in which he lives. He cannot fail to reason that there must be something wrong in a system which affords such unequal distribution of the wealth created by labour.

19 The birth of the Labour Party

In 1889 a book was published which shook the complacency even of the well-to-do – *Labour and life of the people of London*. The author, Charles Booth, could not be dismissed as a Socialist crackpot; he was a wealthy Conservative businessman. He estimated that it was impossible for a family of five to support a minimum standard of health on less than £1 a week. After several years of thorough and careful research, he found that 32 per cent of the people of London, the world's richest city, were living at or below this 'poverty line'. In some districts the figure was 60 per cent.

Booth's findings were confirmed by a similar survey conducted in York by Seebohm Rowntree, the chocolate manufacturer. And in 1903 Rowntree revealed that in rural areas nearly half the labourers were living in a state of sub-human poverty on an average wage of 18s. a week. He concluded that a quarter of Britain's families received 25s. a week or less; about £5 in modern money.

The physical effects of such poverty were appalling. In 1889 nearly half the children of unskilled workers died before the age of five. Those that survived were weak and stunted. During the Boer War (1889–1902) the minimum height for soldiers had to be reduced from 5 ft 3 in to 5 ft. Even then 40 per cent of the recruits were rejected as physically unfit.

The fate of the elderly poor was wretched. One union leader said, 'After fifty the work-

17 *A London night shelter for destitute men, 1910*

man trembles at the thought of his future. Each grey hair is a deadly enemy of his livelihood.' At least the union man might get a small pension; non-unionists and women got nothing. In 1901, the year Queen Victoria died, one person in every five ended his days in the workhouse, the pauper hospital or the lunatic asylum.

Another particularly miserable group were those who worked in the 'sweated' trades: bakers, tailors, cobblers, shop assistants, and others who had no Factory Acts to protect them and no trade unions to fight for them. In 'sweated' trades, a seven-day week of up to eighty hours was common and child labour was still widely used. The wretched 'sweaters' were quite shamelessly exploited by the wealthy. A society lady would think nothing of spending £50 on a ball gown, without reflecting, probably without even knowing, that the seamstress who made it only earned half that sum in a whole year.

Britain was by far the richest country there had ever been. She possessed the largest empire in history and had in 1904 a total national income of £1,710 million. Out of a population of 43 million, 5 million got nearly half of this, and the remaining 38 million got the rest. £200 million went to people with incomes of over £5,000 a year. Little was done to even things up through taxation. For most of the period 1880–1914, income tax was below 1s. in the pound and death duties were extremely light. Yet profits were rising as never before, bringing huge fortunes to the privileged few.

There were some people amongst the comfortable classes who felt ashamed of

18 *James Keir Hardie*

this gross inequality. After the reports of Booth and Rowntree there was a remarkable increase in sympathy for the workers. The old myth that people were only poor through drink, gambling and bad management was exploded. Many people were poor because they were not paid enough to live on, even if they never wasted a penny.

A number of politicians (including the young Winston Churchill) felt that radical changes were needed. They proposed higher taxes for the rich, a standard minimum for wages and a maximum for hours, unemployment and sickness benefit, and old age pensions. But many trade unionists were not prepared to wait for the Liberals and Conservatives to act. They wanted a political party of their own to speak for the underdog, and perhaps one day to take control of the government. The idea had been debated for years, but by the end of the century it was at last nearing fulfilment.

In 1892 a Scottish miner named James Keir Hardie was elected to Parliament as member for West Ham. The House of Commons had grown used to working-class members, but not to ones like Keir Hardie. On the day Parliament opened he drove up in a charabanc accompanied by cheering constituents and a cornet player and wearing a cloth cap. He refused to sit with the Lib/Labs and certainly did not behave like them. During a debate on unemployment he was so shocked by the lack of imagination of other members that he burst out, 'You well-bred beasts!' For three years he terrorised the House with fierce speeches about unemployment, mining accidents and social injustice. Unlike many working-class leaders, he never forgot or forgave the bitter experiences of his youth.

Keir Hardie was born in a one-roomed cottage in a Lanarkshire mining village, where he was reared with eight brothers and sisters. He started work as a baker's errand boy at the age of seven. Once when his parents were ill and he was the only wage-earner in the family, he was given the sack for arriving fifteen minutes late for work. When he was ten he went down the mines. As a young man he became secretary of the Ayrshire Miners Union. In 1888 he founded the Scottish Labour Party, and in 1893 the Independent Labour Party.

At that stage the majority of union leaders preferred their old alliance with the Liberals and were lukewarm about the possibility of a new working-class party. Even for 'new' unionists like Ben Tillet the idea of a Socialist party smacked of the 'hare-brained chatterers and magpies of Continental Revolutionaries'. But Keir Hardie's brand of Socialism was peculiarly British. He was not interested in grand political theories but in practical reforms.

Between 1893 and 1899 the number of Keir Hardie's supporters at the TUC steadily increased, until finally the Parliamentary Committee was persuaded to agree to his plan for a conference to discuss the whole question of Labour representation in Parliament. On February 27 1900, at the Memorial Hall in Farringdon Road, London, the conference met.

It was attended not only by trade-union leaders but by representatives of all existing Socialist organisations, including Hardie's ILP and the Fabian Society. The Fabians were an influential group of middle-class intellectuals. Leading members included well-known writers like George Bernard Shaw, H. G. Wells, William Morris, and Sidney and Beatrice Webb, the historians and instructors of the trade-union movement.

The conference was not particularly dramatic or enthusiastic. Only half the total strength of the TUC was represented, and many of those who attended were somewhat half-hearted. But out of it was born the Labour Representation Committee, in six years time rechristened the Labour Party.

It was not an exclusively trade-union party. Membership was open to any union, Socialist group or sympathetic individual who wished to join. It was a typical British compromise and quite unlike the revolutionary Continental Socialist parties. Its finances were extremely shaky. Member-unions contributed only 10s. per 1,000 members to its funds, and since only a minority of unions joined, the party's income for the first year was a mere £210 10s. 6d. At the 1900 election it could only afford to spend £33 altogether and only two of its candidates were elected, one of whom was Keir Hardie himself. The infant party was still outnumbered by the Lib/Lab group.

In spite of its unspectacular start in life, events were soon to prove that the birth of the Labour Party was the most important event not only in the development of the trade union movement, but also in the history of modern British politics.

20 From Taff Vale to the Osborne Judgement

In August 1900 the signalmen of the Taff Vale railway in Wales came out on strike because one of their number, an active trade unionist, had been downgraded by the company. The men believed that he had been victimised, and they were probably right. Labour relations on the railways were among the worst in all industry. The companies refused to recognise or deal with the unions, claiming that they undermined the strict, almost military, discipline necessary to ensure the safety and reliability of train services. Yet they expected railwaymen to work far longer hours and for less pay than workers in other industries. The average railwayman's wage was 26s. a week, at least 10s. less than the average for a miner or a semi-skilled engineer. Quite often a man might be on duty for between fourteen and eighteen hours at a stretch, a danger both to himself and to passengers. Shunters, whose job was particularly dangerous, were killed at an annual rate of one in two hundred. In view of these appalling conditions and the powerless position of the unions, it is hardly surprising that there were a great many unofficial strikes.

The Taff Vale strike blew up into something much bigger than usual. The general manager of the company, Ammon Beesley, was a quarrelsome, determined man who saw his chance to squash the union. Straight away he advertised for non-union labour and provoked the Amalgamated Society of Railway Servants into making the strike official. When the union pickets tried to turn away the blacklegs, he applied to a judge for a Court Order to stop the picketing, which was granted. He also sued the ASRS for damages — compensation for losses suffered as a result of the strike — and won his case before the highest court in the land, the House of Lords. The union had to pay £42,000 in damages and legal costs.

This case shattered the trade-unions' legal position, which most lawyers thought had been settled by the Acts of 1871 and 1876. As before in union history, the employers had found a loop-hole in the labour laws through which to fire pot-shots at the unions. The Taff Vale decision obviously made strikes practically impossible. Picketing seemed to be once more illegal and any striking union ran the risk of a huge fine. As a result, union leaders discouraged official strikes, and tried instead to improve methods of negotiation and conciliation. There was little else they could do until the law was reversed, and that was a political matter.

After Taff Vale many union leaders woke up to the need for a strong political party. The LRC, at first treated with indifference, was now seen as the main hope of the unions. In 1900 it had only 353,000 affiliated trade-union members; by 1903 it had nearly a million. Most of the major unions joined and agreed to pay a levy of 1d. a year per member into a parliamentary fund for election expenses and the payment of MPs in preparation for the battle ahead.

19 Punch *cartoon, 24 January 1906*
Balfour: *Here, I say! Help! What on earth is it? Another of these awful Labour members?*
Campbell-Bannerman: *Not exactly, my dear Arthur; this is just a clean sweep!*

The 1905 election resulted in a spectacular Liberal victory, after ten years of Conservative government. The trade-unions had high hopes of the new Prime Minister, Sir Henry Campbell-Bannerman, who had shown sympathy for their cause. He certainly presented a contrast to his predecessor, the languid aristocrat Arthur Balfour, who was once reported as asking wearily, 'by the way, what exactly *is* a trade union?'

Due partly to an electoral pact with the Liberals, 56 Labour candidates were successful, 40 of them trade unionists. 29 were LRC men and the rest were Lib/Labs. Never before had Labour been so strongly represented in Parliament. As a mark of this strength the LRC renamed itself the 'Labour Party'.

The government was quick to fulfill the most important promise made during the election campaign, a promise to which they owed thousands of working class votes. In 1906 they passed a Trade Disputes Act which restored completely the freedom to strike and the right of peaceful picketing. This law still applies today.

The years between 1906 and 1911 brought a remarkable spate of social reforms. Taken one by one they were fairly modest, but added together they proved that the old Liberal prejudice against government interference in people's lives was weakening. Reluctantly, Liberals realised that bad health, bad housing, poverty and unemployment undermined the prosperity of the nation and should be corrected by the state. They did not believe as the Socialists did that everyone had the *right* to a decent standard of living, but that people should be allowed to help themselves. This was the guiding principle behind Lloyd George's National Insurance Act of 1911. Each worker had 4d. a week deducted from his wages, which entitled him to benefits when sick or unemployed. The state and his employer also contributed. Socialists fiercely opposed compulsory insurance deductions from workers' wages because they believed that it was the responsibility of the state alone to provide for its needy members. But most trade unions welcomed National Insurance, especially as they were made partly responsible for distributing the benefits.

The Labour Party, including its Socialist members, found less to complain of in the rest of the government's social legislation, except of course that it was not enough. It provided free school meals for needy children, old age pensions for the poorest over-seventies, and compensation for workers who had suffered injury or illness through their work. Labour Exchanges were opened with lists of vacancies for men seeking work, and public relief work was provided for some of the unemployed. Moreover, Lloyd George's 'People's Budget' of 1909 skimmed more money from the rich than ever before.

Also, under pressure from the Labour Party and the unions, several important industrial Acts were passed. The miners' working day was limited to eight hours at the coalface, and pit safety regulations were greatly improved. Minimum wages were fixed for the worst-paid 'sweated' trades, and shop-assistants were given a half-holiday.

So far so good. It seemed as if the Labour Party could just sit back and wait for its Liberal friends to grant its wishes one by one. But in 1910 the interest of the Liberal government in labour matters began to cool. The new Prime Minister, Mr Asquith, was a more orthodox old-style Liberal than Campbell-Bannerman, and the majority of Liberals disliked anything that smacked of Socialism. They thought that they had done quite enough for the underdog already, and that the state should not shoulder any more responsibility for the welfare of private citizens. Also, the Labour Party was hardly in a position to make trouble. After the election of 1910, they and the Irish members held the balance between the Conservatives and the Liberals, so that if they voted against the government they risked bringing the Conservatives back. Therefore, partly out of political necessity and partly out of habit they had become, under Ramsay MacDonald's leadership, almost a tame junior branch of the Liberal Party. The government could afford to take their support for granted and ignore their demands.

The weakness of their position was made embarrassingly obvious by the Osborne Judgement, a case almost as serious as Taff Vale. In 1909, Walter Osborne, a branch secretary of the Amalgamated Society of Railway Servants, challenged the right of trade unions to raise subscriptions for the Labour Party. He was a Liberal, and quite reasonably did not see why Liberal and Conservative trade unionists should pay a compulsory levy. His case went to the House of Lords and the levy was declared illegal. Suddenly the Labour Party was stripped of its main source of income. In spite of Labour's pleas, the Osborne judgement was not reversed until 1913, and even then there were strings attached. Political and benefit funds were to be kept separate, and any unionist who objected to the political levy could 'contract out' of paying it. It was a fair compromise, but nonetheless a blow to Labour.

21 The Labour unrest of 1910-14

The history of the trade-union movement falls into a rough pattern of alternating periods of patient plodding, and excited activity and expansion, which more or less follow the ups and downs of the economic situation. Between 1870 and 1875 there was a great spurt forward, followed by a slow plod through the Great Depression. The revival of trade in 1888 helped to unleash the gas and dock strikes and the 'New' unskilled unions. This upheaval was again followed by a quiet patch between 1900 and 1910. Then came five years of furious conflict, 1910–14.

In the five years before the First World War, over twice as many workers were involved in strikes and lock-outs as in the first ten years of the twentieth century. Almost every industry in Britain from mining to onion-pickling was affected. Even the London music-halls were silenced for a while by a strike of comedians and musicians. Trade unions sprang up amongst the most unlikely groups, such as teachers, shop-assistants and clerks. Unskilled workers, including agricultural labourers, became better organised. Total membership leapt to a record of over 4 million. Between 1900 and 1910 it had risen by only half a million; between 1910 and 1914 it rose by over one and a half million.

The contrast between the two periods cannot be explained entirely in economic terms. Between 1901 and 1906 the unions had been partially paralysed by the Taff Vale ruling, and smothered by the moderate character of the majority of their leaders. Also, much of their steam had been diverted into the Labour Party after its success in the 1905 election, because hopes of progress were pinned on political rather than industrial action.

But by 1910 many trade unions had lost faith in the Labour Party and were openly scornful of the mild leadership of Ramsay MacDonald. In spite of the Liberal government's reforms, the workers' share in the country's wealth was falling. Wages had stuck still for over twenty years whereas prices had risen steeply. Wage-earners were actually worse off in 1910 than they had been in 1890.

Obviously the restraint of the union leaders had not paid off, either in higher wages or in increased respect from the employers. They still had to haggle like disgruntled servants with their masters. Although there were a few far-sighted employers who tried to avoid disputes by building up the authority of the unions through regular negotiations and written agreements, the majority were still hostile to collective bargaining. They insisted on their right to hire non-union as well as union men, and to strike individual bargains when they wished. Some employers, like the railway companies, refused to recognise the unions or have any dealings with them.

Many younger radical unionists were naturally impatient with this state of affairs and were ready for militant action, if necessary in defiance of the official leader-

20 *Masked members of the National Union of Clerks, September 1913*

21 *Tom Mann*

ship. They were attracted by the ideas of an extremist group called the Syndicalists, led by Tom Mann, one of the heroes of the 1889 Dock Strike. In 1910 Mann arrived back from a tour abroad, convinced that British workers should follow the examples of French and American unions and launch all-out class warfare. According to his plan for Direct Action, groups of militants would stage a series of lightning strikes in key industries. Then, once the employers' resistance was worn down, all unions would join together for a general strike. After the surrender of the capitalists, the workers would take over industry and the government.

D

An essential step along Mann's path to revolution was a complete reorganisation of the unions. There was certainly plenty of scope. In 1909 there were 1,100 unions representing 22 million workers; that is, about one union for every 19,000 workers. In the building trade alone there were 19 major unions and numerous small local ones. There was rivalry and confusion everywhere. Craft and general labourers' unions quarrelled amongst themselves and with each other over who should join what union, and whose members should do what jobs and work what machines. Mann believed in huge 'industrial' unions on the American pattern, covering all the workers in each industry. Eventually he hoped for just one big union.

Even in the explosive atmosphere of 1910, such foreign revolutionary schemes made little headway amongst British trade unions. Ambitious amalgamations were usually blocked by loyalty to existing unions. Even the Transport Workers' Federation of seamen, drivers and dockers, started in 1910 by Mann himself, was rather a loose, ramshackle affair. The nearest thing in Britain to an 'industrial' union was the National Union of Railwaymen, formed in 1913, but it was not particularly syndicalist in character.

As the labour unrest gathered force, the government and employers imagined that they could see the red hand of Tom Mann behind every strike. In fact, except amongst the South Wales miners, committed syndicalists were noisy but not numerous. Most unionists were not interested in seizing political power or destroying capitalism — they were simply fighting for better pay and conditions. Manual workers were better educated than their fathers had been and had higher expectations. They were sick of crowded slums, second-hand clothes, and bread and margarine.

The industrial troubles of 1910 reached an ugly climax in the autumn during a dispute in the South Wales coalfields. 30,000 miners were out on strike in support of a demand for fairer payment for men who had to work in 'abnormal places' — deep and rocky pits where the coal was hard to cut. At the beginning of November fighting broke out in the village of Ton-y-pandy after the arrival of a gang of blacklegs. For several days there was a series of pitched battles in the village streets. Policemen were punched and stoned, and strikers were battered with truncheons. In the nearby village of Aberainon, a number of bystanders, including several children, were beaten and thrown into the canal by policemen, and at Ton-y-pandy one striker was killed in a scuffle. The Chief Constable of Glamorgan sent an urgent demand to the Home Secretary, Winston Churchill, for reinforcements. Within two days a combined force of London policemen and cavalry arrived, under the command of General Macready. The general acted with admirable impartiality and skill, and soon restored order.

The original dispute, however, was still unsettled, and the strike dragged on for another eight months, until the miners were starved back to work. It left painful scars which did not heal for many years. Ton-y-pandy, like Tolpuddle, became part of the bitter folk-lore of the Labour movement.

1911 was Tom Mann's busiest year. In June a dispute flared up between the Seamen's Union and the shipowners over pay and conditions. The shipowners were fiercely anti-union and refused to negotiate. They hoped to provoke a strike, smash it by sending shiploads of blacklegs to the ports, and ruin the unions. Quite the opposite happened. On June 20th seamen at Southampton, Goole and Hull came out on strike. Encouraged by the Transport Workers Federation, the dockers at Hull came out in sympathy. By August all the major ports except London were tangled up. The employers' shiploads of blacklegs sailed from port to port but were turned away by pickets.

The Board of Trade conciliator, a patient and flexible man called George Askwith, scurried from one trouble spot to the next. In Hull he was greeted by hysterical town councillors and equally hysterical dockers' wives. In Manchester he spent a week in the Town Hall where 18 transport unions were debating with 18 groups of employers about 18 different disputes. Askwith settled them all, mainly in favour of the strikers.

No sooner had he arrived back in London than he was drawn into an even more serious battle between the Transport Workers Federation and the Port of London Authority. The problems were recognition of the Federation and its member-unions, and pay and conditions for several groups of workers. For Ben Tillett, the leader of the 1889 strike, it was just like old times, with processions through dockland and mass meetings on Tower Hill. Tempers were kept aflame by a long heatwave, and to add to the chaos thousands of women workers poured out of the East End factories. Jam-makers, sweet-wrappers and glue-mixers paraded through the streets, shouting and singing and generally alarming respectable people. Altogether there were twenty such strikes, eighteen of which were victorious. The dock strike was eventually settled when Mr Askwith persuaded the employers to meet most of the strikers' demands, including a rise in their hourly rate from 6d. to 8d.

Meanwhile, in Liverpool, Tom Mann was stirring up fresh trouble. An unofficial strike of local railwaymen gave him an opportunity to call a 'sympathetic' supporting strike of dockside and transport workers in the name of the Transport Workers Federation. The entire transport system ground to a halt, food ran out, and the city was thrown almost into a state of siege. Extra police and soldiers were sent in to deal with riots. On one occasion troops opened fire on the crowd; on another, an angry group of strikers set fire to the Town Hall. Eventually the City Council had to give in. Most of the strikers' demands were granted and they were given back their old jobs.

22 *Rioting in Liverpool, August 1911. Police rounding up demonstrators.*

By that time, however, groups of railwaymen all over the country were coming out on unofficial strikes. The leaders of the four main railway unions held an urgent meeting, declared the strikes official, and demanded immediate negotiations with the railway companies. In spite of an appeal from the Prime Minister, the employers refused to recognise the unions. On August 17th the unions sent telegrams to all local branches, saying: 'Your liberty is at stake. All railwaymen must strike at once. The loyalty of each means victory for all.'

Although many railwaymen stayed at work, the strike that followed was big enough to disorganise all train-services. The government was so alarmed that it sent troops to all main railway centres. The strikers jumped to the conclusion that they had come to protect blacklegs and perhaps even to run the trains. In some areas this provoked violence. In Llanelly in Wales they threw such a barrage of stones and bottles at the troops that the officer in charge commanded his men to fire. Two strikers were killed, one wounded, and the crowd fled in terror. In revenge the strikers looted trucks and set them on fire. Unfortunately they were filled with explosives and blew up. Four people were killed and many injured.

Violence on this scale was quite common in America and in some European countries, but so far Britain had normally managed to avoid it. Luckily, at this dangerous moment the sight of blood shocked the government into forcing a compromise. Lloyd George, the Chancellor of the Exchequer, persuaded the employers to grant enough of the railway-

23 *Durham miners photographed underground the day before the strike. March 1912.*

men's demands to end the strike. The railway companies grudgingly agreed to deal indirectly with the union through Conciliation Boards, but balked at full recognition. It was only a partial victory for the railwaymen.

Intervention by the government in the settlement of industrial disputes was a fairly recent development. In the past the government's role had been limited to the maintenance of order, while the employers and unions fought it out. But confronted by strikes on an ever larger scale which threatened to bring transport and industry to a standstill, the government was forced to take a more active part. One Board of Trade Conciliator, however hard-working, was no longer enough. Between 1910 and 1914 the government, even the Prime Minister himself, were dragged deeper and deeper into the battle between Capital and Labour.

On March 1st 1912 more than a million miners stopped work. It was the biggest strike the country had yet experienced. Within a week the coal shortage had seriously affected the railways and factories. The Prime Minister Mr Asquith called a meeting of miners and mine-owners, but the two sides only glared at each other. The Miners Federation wanted a national wage of 5s. per shift for men and 2s. for boys. The employers insisted on the right of each district, even of each colliery, to fix its own wage rates. They rejected the idea of a minimum wage, whether at national or district level.

In desperation Mr Asquith decided to force the employers to come to terms by rushing a Miners' Minimum Wage Act through Parliament. When he rose to speak in the House his face was trembling, 'We have exhausted all our powers of argument and negotiation', he began. He searched for the next words but they would not come. And then Members saw that the Prime Minister was in tears. This industrial crisis, on top of the violent 'Votes for Women' campaign of the suffragettes, the struggle over Home Rule for Ireland, and the growing threat of war with Germany, had broken his self-control.

The Miners' Wage Act was passed and on April 6th the Miners Federation took a ballot of its members. Because there was only a small majority in favour of continuing, the strike was called off. The employers had been forced to accept the principle of district minimum wages, though the rates they fixed fell far short of the miners' demands.

24 *The London transport strike, May 1912. Police escorting meat vans from Smithfield market.*

25 *Ben Tillet addressing a strike meeting on Tower Hill, 1912*

The last big strike of 1912 — there were many other small ones — was a victory for the employers. The Port of London Authority under the determined leadership of Lord Devonport had its revenge on the Transport Workers Federation. Following a dispute about the use of non-union labour, the TWF called a general strike throughout the ports. But this time provincial workers did not respond and the strike was a flop. Ben Tillett's ferocious prayer, 'God strike Lord Devonport dead!' was not answered. The TWF suffered a humiliating defeat and many of its members were sacked.

In 1913 the scene of battle moved to Ireland. Ireland, which was still under British rule, was a desperately poor country. There was continual mass unemployment and wages were miserably low. The slums of Dublin were the worst in Britain.

The smouldering bitterness of years of misery exploded in August 1913 into a series of strikes and lockouts. The workers struck not only against their employers but also indirectly against the exploitation of Ireland by the English. The Irish Transport Workers Federation, besides being a huge industrial union, was also an important force in the fight for Ireland's independence. Its leaders, Jim Larkin and James Connelly, were famous Irish patriots. They were fighting employers who were not only ruthless enemies of organised labour, but also allies of the English rulers.

The brutality used by the police and soldiers against the strikers aroused fierce indignation amongst English trade unionists. Ton-y-pandy, Liverpool and Llanelly were small affairs in comparison with the Dublin street-fights. Several men were killed and hundreds beaten up, including many women and children.

Larkin appealed to English trade unions to stage sympathetic strikes, but their leaders rejected the idea as impractical and confined their support to supplies of food and money. The TUC tried to mediate, but the Irish employers were set on total victory. Early in 1914 they crushed the strike, but the Irish TWF lived to fight another day.

22 The Triple Alliance

The strike fever of 1910–14 turned the trade-union movement inside out. At first many leaders tried to keep their impatient members in check, but the pressure proved too strong for them. More and more often they were forced to give official backing to spontaneous unofficial strikes. In some unions moderate leaders were voted down by the rank and file and replaced by militants. In others the established leaders themselves adopted a tougher official policy. At the 1911 TUC one formerly cautious elderly leader declared, 'Let those strike who have never struck before, and those who have always struck, strike all the more.'

The conflict between moderates and militants was echoed in the labour press. The provocative *Daily Herald*, which started in 1911 as a strike bulletin, fanned the flames of discontent, while the sober *Daily Citizen*, the mouthpiece of the Labour Party and TUC, tried in vain to smother them. The *Herald* exactly caught the mood of exhilaration which was sweeping through the rank and file. They felt that at last they had the government and the employers on the run. Many more strikes were successful than in previous years; militant action was obviously paying off.

One tonic effect of militancy was to draw the unions closer together. This was particularly noticeable among the railwaymen. The 1911 strike had forced the weak and divided railway unions to co-operate. In 1913 three unions amalgamated into a new National Union of Railwaymen. The drivers and footplatemen stuck to their own union, but the rest of the industry's manual workers joined the NUR. Within a year it had grown into one of the largest and strongest unions in Britain.

The trade-union movement was now dominated by three giants: the NUR, the Miners' Federation and the Transport Workers Federation. In 1913 their executive committees decided to put flesh onto the old union motto, 'Unity is Strength', by forming a Triple Alliance. Their experience in recent strikes had shown how closely involved they already were in each other's affairs.

26
National Union of Railwaymen banner, 1919

A stoppage in any one of these key industries affected workers in the other two. A coal strike, for instance, caused temporary unemployment on the railways and docks. There was also the question of sympathetic action — strikes or 'go-slows', embargoes on the movement of goods, and the prevention of blacklegging. The Triple Alliance was designed to solve these practical problems by preventing one of the 'big three' from embarking on a strike without consulting the other two.

The Alliance had another more ambitious purpose. The three unions planned that they would all present simultaneous demands to the employers, and that each would refuse a settlement until the other two agreed. They hoped that the threat of a triple strike would frighten the employers into surrender.

This plan held terrible dangers for the government. It meant that the strike might be used as a political weapon to ruin capitalist industry and launch Tom Mann's promised revolution. There were some firebrands in the Alliance who wanted exactly that, but most of the leaders were less extreme. Although in the long term they hoped to abolish private ownership of their respective industries, their immediate purpose was simply to raise the living standards of their members.

In the event the Triple Alliance was not put to the test for several years. Like all other trade-union activities it was cut short by the declaration of war with Germany in 1914.

56

23 The First World War

On Sunday August 2nd 1914 a huge crowd of trade unionists and labour supporters gathered in Trafalgar Square to demonstrate against the approaching war. They cheered the International Labour slogans, 'Down with class rule! Down with the war! Up with the peaceful rule of the people!' On the next day Germany invaded Belgium, and on August 4th Britain declared war.

Although the Labour Party was divided in its attitude, the trade-union movement was immediately carried away by patriotic feelings. Its leaders felt that their first duty was to help the government win the war. Strikers went straight back to work, and several unions, including the engineers, withdrew their pay-claims. The TUC declared an Industrial Truce which banned official strikes as long as the war lasted. This was an unselfish patriotic gesture because it was made before any promises were received from the employers.

The unions also helped the government in their recruiting campaign. Thousands of volunteers enlisted with the armed forces. Many were skilled men with good jobs, but others were low paid workers who may have seen the army as an escape from a life of drudgery. The army doctors were horrified by the poor physical condition of these slum dwellers; in 1916 41 per cent of the recruits were rejected as unfit.)

At first nearly everyone thought the war would only last a few months. The railways were immediately brought under state control but little else was done to reorganise industry. The motto was, 'business as usual'. The result was chaos. Prices rose sharply, there was an appalling shortage of shells and weapons, and many factories lost large numbers of workers to the army. The government would obviously have to take a firmer grip.

In July 1915 Lloyd George, as Minister of Munitions, passed an Act applying to all industries engaged in war work. Strikes were made illegal and arbitration in industrial disputes was made compulsory. Trade unions were forced to suspend all rules and restrictions which held back production, such as limits on overtime, and to accept the 'dilution' of labour – the use of women and unskilled workers in jobs usually reserved for craftsmen. So the unions had to sacrifice many of their hard-won privileges for the sake of the country.

In return the government promised to restore union rights after the war and to make sure returning soldiers got their old jobs back. The unions' qualms were further settled when the government took over the mines and shipyards and imposed a special tax on the increased profits of firms making war supplies.

At the very beginning of the war Mr Asquith had invited the leader of the Labour Party, Arthur Henderson, to join the government, because it was obvious that the co-operation of the unions would be vital to the war effort. In 1916 Lloyd George became Prime Minister of an all-party Coalition. He

27 *Women war workers in an engineering shop, 1914–18*

immediately brought more Labour men into the government and gave more responsibility to the unions. Union officials of all ranks sat on committees concerned with recruitment, the supply of skilled men, and the production of war supplies. This gave them valuable experience and boosted their self-confidence.

But the closer they worked with the government the wider became the gap between them and their ordinary members. This was especially serious in the engineering and shipbuilding industries which were most affected by the war. Production was greatly increased, and large numbers of new workers brought in. Although the employers had promised to pay them the usual rate for the job, they rarely did. The unlimited demand for war supplies brought them immense profits which the government's tax barely scratched. Many huge fortunes were made. Naturally the engineers were enraged, especially in Scotland where unionists had always been particularly militant.

In 1915 and 1916 there were several fierce unofficial strikes on Clydeside. They were led by local leaders called 'shop stewards' — unpaid officials of the ASE responsible for union affairs at factory and workshop level. During the war, shop stewards became much more important and powerful, partly because the top leaders could not cope with all the new problems caused by the war, and partly because they were fiery men of action with a strong popular following. Eventually the government solved the Clydeside problem by arresting the ringleaders, but by the end of the war the shop-steward movement was causing trouble in other industries as well.

During the last year of the war there was a rash of unofficial strikes which severely strained the Industrial Truce. There were several reasons for the workers' growing discontent. The first was simply weariness at the miseries of conscription and the terrible slaughter of young men. Many trade unionists thought that Britain could and should have made peace in 1917, and the top Labour leaders resigned from the government on this question. Some of the 1918 strikes were led by men who hoped to force the government into peace talks. They wanted to follow the lead of the Russian revolutionaries who, in 1917, overthrew their government and withdrew from the 'capitalists' war'.

But the most pressing reason was the rising cost of living. Prices doubled during the war, and although the government paid several 'war bonuses' to many groups of workers, wages always lagged behind. As one railwayman wrote, 'To see one's wife growing paler and thinner through lack of nourishing food makes me pause and wonder whether it is possible to carry patriotism too far.'

Yet in spite of the growing unrest towards the end of the war, the co-operation between the government and the trade unions was a success. As Lloyd George admitted later:

Had Labour been hostile the war would not have been carried on effectively. Had Labour been lukewarm, victory would have been secured with increasing difficulty.

24 Lloyd George and labour

Amid the rejoicing at the end of that long and terrible war it seemed as if the bitterness of the old class struggles might at last be forgotten and forgiven, and that a fairer, more tolerant society might be built. Certainly the need for industrial peace and progress was urgent. Britain's share in world trade was falling year by year. Her old-fashioned industries needed a thorough overhaul to enable them to stand up to massive competition from America. If only unions, employers and government could work in moderate harmony for a few years, the prosperity everyone desired might be achieved. But could they?

Immediately after the war the prospects looked good. The advantages to unions and employers alike of co-operation and consultation had been demonstrated during the war, and moderate men on both sides were anxious not to return to the free-for-all. Besides, two of the unions' most cherished desires had been fulfilled during the war: national rather than local wage-bargaining in many industries, and state control of the mines and railways. They had moreover been led to believe that these changes would be permanent.

The government made several other promising gestures. In November 1918 it

28 *Policemen on strike, August 1919*

passed an Act forbidding wage reductions for one year. It also kept its pledge to restore pre-war trade-union rules and regulations. Efforts were also made to civilise wage-bargaining through Industrial Courts and (for government employees) through Whitley Councils on which both employers and unions were represented.

For a few months it looked as if common-sense and moderation would prevail. But the opportunity was thrown away. Old prejudices re-appeared, old mistakes were repeated; and while the economy sickened, the opposing forces of capital and labour stumbled into a series of bitter conflicts which culminated in the General Strike of 1926. During the three years 1919–21 there were far more strikes than in the worst pre-war years of 1910–13. Even the police went on strike in London and Liverpool over the right to form a union.

The most immediate cause of labour unrest was inflation. Prices, which had doubled during the war, continued to rise so steeply that by July 1920 £1 would buy only as much as 7s. 6d. in 1914. Naturally the unions pressed for matching increases in wages and if necessary went on strike to get them. But wages always lagged behind, leaving many workers worse off than they had been before the war.

Manufacturers and speculators made the situation worse by grabbing quick profits, instead of investing in the future of industry. The government made little effort to control either prices or profits. As a result, when the post-war boom collapsed early in 1921 the crash was more sudden and serious than it need have been.

In this feverish atmosphere the unions grew more aggressive and impatient. Between 1914 and 1920 their membership doubled to a record of over 8 million. They felt that the time was ripe to test their strength, to let fly with all the demands they had bottled up during the war. Now the brakes of patriotism and war regulations were released, they presented the employers with a series of demands not just for more money and shorter hours, but for public ownership of various industries and more workers' control. The Russian Revolution of 1917 and the post-war German revolution encouraged their belief that they might be able to force sweeping social and political change in Britain.

Surprisingly, their only real political victory was over foreign policy. In August 1920 some London dockers refused to load a ship called the *Jolly George* with armaments for

Poland, which was at war with Soviet Russia. The government was on the brink of joining the war on Poland's side and the unions were determined to stop it. They believed, rightly, that the majority of British people were against another war, and that the workers would refuse to fight against the Russian revolutionaries. So they formed Councils of Action to organise resistance, and threatened a general strike if war was declared. Undoubtedly this threat was the main reason why Lloyd George hastily withdrew his support from the anti-Communist armies. He was well aware of the strength of left-wing sentiment. 'Europe is filled with revolutionary ideas,' he said. 'A feeling of passion and revolt reigns in the breast of the working class.'

During the war Lloyd George had often expressed sympathy with the workers' aspirations. He even told the turbulent Clydeside strikers, 'Boys, I'm as keen a Socialist as any of you.' But now he changed his tune. He became Prime Minister of a coalition government in which Conservatives far outnumbered Liberals both in Parliament and in the Cabinet, and he bent his principles and his policies to suit them. Moreover the majority of Conservative members were businessmen, described by the future prime minister, Stanley Baldwin, as 'hard-faced men who looked as if they had done well out of the war'.

Lloyd George had saved Britain in 1916, but after the war his devious behaviour added fuel to the flames of industrial unrest. Moreover he destroyed the Liberal Party by joining the Conservatives, leaving Labour as the only real opposition party. Unfortunately, with only 59 Labour MPs facing 479 Coalitionists, it was too weak either to influence the government or to moderate the ambitions and activities of the trade unions, which had stolen the political initiative from it.

It was the government's handling of the two great state-controlled industries which irretrievably poisoned its relations with the trade unions. Lloyd George was in a delicate position, for although he had little sympathy with the employers, especially the mine-owners, he had pawned his political future to the Conservatives. So he played a double game. He reassured his new allies that the mines and railways would be handed back to their previous owners, while pretending to the unions that the issue was still in the balance.

In January 1919 the Miners' Federation demanded a 30 per cent wage increase, shorter hours and nationalisation. As with most union claims this was probably more than they expected to get, even though coal had made immense profits since 1914. Lloyd George warded off the threatened strike by appointing a Royal Commission to inquire into the coal industry. Its membership was fairly balanced: three leading miners, three pro-Labour economists, three coal-owners and three other industrialists, under the chairmanship of a judge, Sir John Sankey. For three months the Commission virtually held the mine-owners in the dock, and the case went against them. In May it recommended a compromise settlement on wages and hours, and decided by a majority of one vote (the chairman's) in favour of nationalisation. It said bluntly: 'The present system of ownership stands condemned', and recommended 'that the principle of state ownership of the coalmines be accepted.' Furthermore it said, 'it is in the interests of the country that the colliery workers shall in the future have an effective voice in the direction of the mine'.

The government, having already promised to accept the Report in spirit and in letter, proceeded to ignore it, protesting that the members of the Commission had been divided. So the miners had cancelled their strike for nothing. Their leaders moaned, 'We have been deceived, betrayed, duped.'

It was the railwaymen's turn next. When the NUR presented its claims in September, one of the railway directors, Lord Claud Hamilton, urged the government to 'take off the velvet gloves they had worn too long.' Lloyd George took his advice. Big cuts in wages for all NUR grades were announced, while in a cunning attempt to divide the railwaymen, increases were granted to ASLEF, the drivers' union. The ruse failed, because on September 26th the drivers came out on strike in support of the NUR. After eight days the government was forced to compromise on wages and hours. But two years later it dropped its plans to nationalise and electrify the railways, and handed them back to private ownership.

In October 1920 there was another mining strike over wages and coal prices. After the NUR had threatened a sympathetic strike, the government made with the Miners Federation a temporary settlement which included a small pay rise and the promise of a National Wages Board. But at the same time it armed itself against future disputes by passing the Emergency Powers Act. This meant that if ever essential public services were disrupted, the government could arrest troublemakers, and use troops and volunteers to take over from strikers, without reference to Parliament. It granted to the Cabinet powers which had only previously been needed in time of war. Obviously the government expected trouble.

In fact it invited trouble. In February 1921 it announced that the mines would be decontrolled on March 31st and airily told the mine-owners and the Miners Federation to work out their own future. But the gap between the two was hopelessly wide. The Federation was determined never to return to the old system of district wage-rates under which men working at poor collieries got far less than men in prosperous ones. They wanted a National Pool to equalise profits and wages. The owners, dominated by a few rich magnates, were so set on district arrangements, that they refused even to discuss the matter. Furthermore they quickly

29 *The coal crisis of 1921. A strike meeting in Wigan.*

announced the new district rates which were nearly all far below existing levels. The worst area was South Wales where some men faced cuts of up to half their wages.

Admittedly the coal industry was having a lean time; exports were falling and the government subsidies were drying up. But these cuts were cruelly unfair, especially since the owners wrung a promise from the government to maintain the existing profit-level for a year. The miners were expected to pay the whole price for the decline of the industry, even though the main reason for this decline was inefficient management, as the Sankey Commission had proved.

On decontrol day, March 31st 1921, over a million miners were locked-out. The Miners Federation appealed to the Triple Alliance for help, the NUR and transport workers decided to embargo the movement of coal from Saturday April 16th. But they insisted, as the price for their support, that negotiations should be re-opened with the owners. They did not relish taking sympathetic action because many of their members earned less than the miners and were far more vulnerable than them to the government's strike-breaking powers.

The Triple Alliance's threat stirred the government into belated action. It re-entered the negotiations and together with the moderate rail and transport leaders tried to narrow the gap between miners and owners. But at the same time it declared a State of Emergency, mobilised the reserves and turned London's parks into Army camps.

The day before the embargo was due to begin, the Miners' secretary, Frank Hodges, hinted that his Federation might temporarily accept district settlements provided the government and owners made some concessions. The transport leaders and the government welcomed this, but the Miners' executive snubbed Hodges and by a majority of one voted to continue the strike. The transport leaders, dismayed by the obstinacy, secrecy and disunity of the Miners Federation called off their embargo. The miners, left to face a grim three-month strike, ending in crushing defeat, branded the transport leaders as traitors. April 15th 1921 became thereafter known as Black Friday.

Although these events caused great bitterness and killed the already moribund Triple Alliance for good, the embargo would probably have been a failure anyway, because only a small majority of railwaymen and transport workers supported it. Also the economic situation of the country had taken a sharp turn for the worse and the unions were all driven back on the defensive.

63

25 The Slump and unemployment

By the late summer of 1920 the brief post-war boom had started to fade. Prices fell, factories closed down and the number of men out of work rose steadily. By June 1921 it had reached 2 million. J. R. Clynes, a trade-union leader and Labour MP, later recalled his horror at seeing so many 'ragged men begging in the gutters in the remnants of khaki overcoats.'

At first they were angry and active. They marched and demonstrated and were hustled about by the police. On armistice day 1922 the official military procession was followed by a ragged army wearing medals and pawn tickets and carrying a banner which read, 'From the living victims, the unemployed, to our own dead comrades who died in vain.'

Then they sank into apathy. Year followed year and still no jobs. Between the wars unemployment rarely fell below a million, and in 1933, the worst year, it reached three million. It ceased to be regarded as a passing fever and became a chronic disease. Gradually many of the older men lost hope of ever working again, of ever opening another wage-packet. They stopped seeking jobs that did not exist and just drew their unemployment money. In many families the fathers had to cadge pocket-money from their wives and sons. They reached such a state of inward despair and outward shabbiness that even when there were jobs available they were unemployable.

Most of this hard-core unemployment was in the old staple industries like coal, cotton and shipbuilding, industries which were hardest hit by more efficient and modern foreign competition. So the traditional industrial regions in the North and Wales suffered far more than the South where new industries like cars, chemicals and electrical goods were developing. In 1930 Wales had an unemployment rate of 31 per cent compared with 10 per cent in London; the North and Scotland had an average of 26 per cent. Glasgow, Hartlepool, Jarrow, became ghost towns with half the male population permanently unemployed. At regular intervals, processions, of grim-faced men from these miserable towns trudged down the road to London to batter on the government's door. These were the famous Hunger Marches.

The government had continually to extend and change national insurance to cover the long-term unemployed. In 1921 a system of regular payments to those 'genuinely seeking work' and their dependents were started – the Dole, as it was grudgingly called.

Unemployment drained the unions of funds and of members. Between 1920 and 1926 they lost 3 million members. The record 1920 figure of 8 million was not regained until 1942. At first they tried levying working members to provide for those out of work, but as wages were falling this could not be kept up. Because trade was so depressed, the unions failed to raise the living standards of their members, employed or unemployed,

30 *South Wales Hunger Marchers on the way to London, 1932*

31 *Unemployed man in Wigan, November 1939*

and because they failed many members dropped out, which made them even weaker. They were caught in a vicious circle.

From 1934 onwards the economy began to recover at last, and so did union membership. Both the government and the employers were more able and willing to improve the conditions of the working class. There was a general rise in wages and a reduction in working hours. Welfare benefits were increased and extended, and in 1938 8 million workers gained the right to one week's paid holiday a year.

Unfortunately these improvements were confined to the South, and to people with jobs. In the depressed areas heavy industry continued to decline and unemployment was as bad as ever. A new ice-cream factory in Middlesex was no help to an unemployed miner in Durham. The increasing prosperity of some areas and some sections of the population only underlined the hopelessness of others. In 1939 there were still 2 million families living in dire poverty.

Mass unemployment had a profound effect on the Labour movement. It turned many people into temporary Communists. But it also brought into the Labour Party a number of sympathetic middle-class people, including two of its future leaders, Clement Attlee and Hugh Gaitskell. It deepened the trade unionists' distrust of capitalist industry and of the bosses. To this day the attitudes of many older trade unionists are coloured by bitter memories of the poverty, boredom and humiliation of those years.

Yet such was the general improvement in the working-class standard of living during the twentieth century that even an unemployed man in the 1930s was better off than an unskilled labourer in 1900. The men who passed through the recruiting offices in 1939, even men who had lived for years on the dole, were far better physical specimens than the generation of 1914.

26 The General Council and the First Labour Government

Although the slump blunted the unions' bargaining power, it did spur them to make some necessary improvements in their organisation. From 1919 onwards several important amalgamations took place: The Iron and Steel Association, The Amalgamated Engineering Union, The National Union of General and Municipal Workers, and The Transport and General Workers Union, which became, under the forceful leadership of Ernest Bevin, the largest union in Britain.

The series of big disputes which led up to Black Friday revealed the urgent need for better co-operation and leadership. The Triple Alliance collapsed because its policies were vague, its procedure slapdash and its members quarrelsome. The transport unions had been particularly infuriated by the way that the Miners Federation expected them to bring a million men out on strike without allowing them any part in the negotiations.

Bevin described the trade-union movement in 1919 as 'a great shapeless mass'. He insisted that, 'if there is going to be unity in action there must be unity in counsel.' He suggested a permanent committee to co-ordinate policy, lead negotiations and act as umpire between warring unions. In September 1921 the General Council of the TUC was formed, consisting of thirty members representing groups of unions. It was a sort of trade-union cabinet, but though its functions were wide it had little power to force individual unions to follow its rulings. Its strength depended, and still depends, on the energy, common-sense and popularity of its members, particularly of the General Secretary at its head.

In the 1920s and 1930s the General Council was dominated by moderate men who exercised a steadying influence on the Labour Movement. In particular they guarded it against Communism. Even during the grimmest years of the slump it refused to associate the TUC with Communist activities on behalf of the unemployed. And when the fortunes of the Labour Party had sunk to the lowest depths after 1931, the General Council gave it the resolution to resist the temptation of forming an alliance with the Communists.

Unlike other European Communist parties, the Communist Party of Great Britain failed to capture large sections of the trade-union movement, or to win a mass following. This was largely due to the solidity of British trade unions and the antipathy of the majority of trade unionists to a political creed they regarded as alien and somehow unsavoury.

Between 1919 and 1923 the number of Labour voters and MPs steadily increased. In the December 1923 General Election the Conservatives campaigned on the unpopular issue of import controls and lost their overall majority. Though still the largest single party, they were outnumbered by an opposition of 158 Liberal and 191 Labour MPs. The Liberals, who held the balance, decided to support a Labour government. On January 22nd 1924 Ramsay MacDonald became Prime Minister.

It was an extraordinary moment in British political history. George V wrote in his diary: *Today 23 years ago dear Grandmama died. I wonder what she would have made of a Labour Government!*

The Labour ministers, all but five of whom had no previous experience of government office, felt nervous and exicted as they arrived at Buckingham Palace in their hired court dress. J. R. Clynes the Privy Seal recalled:

As we stood waiting for his Majesty amid the gold and crimson magnificence of the Palace, I could not help marvelling at the strange turn of Fortune's wheel which had brought MacDonald the starveling clerk, Thomas the engine-driver, Henderson the foundry labourer and Clynes the millhand to this pinnacle.

They stayed on this pinnacle only nine months. The need for Liberal support prevented them from attempting any really Socialist measures. Clynes said that the government felt like a long-distance runner with a heavy weight (the Liberal Party) chained to his leg. They did, however, manage to pass a Housing Act which provided for more cheap subsidised houses for rent, and to improve the state school system.

32 *Members of the first Labour Government on the way to Buckingham Palace, January 1924. Left to right: Ramsay MacDonald, J. H. Thomas, Arthur Henderson, J. Clynes.*

The first Labour Government was a great disappointment to most of its supporters. Even had it been politically strong enough to carry out new and bold policies, it probably would not have done so. Ramsay MacDonald himself was no Socialist, and his chief lieutenants, Philip Snowden the Chancellor of the Exchequer, Clynes, Henderson and J. H. Thomas, the railway leader, were all cautious and moderate men with a respect for tradition and orthodox finance. Apart from some welcome changes in the administration of the dole they made no imaginative efforts to improve the depressing economic situation.

Their dealings with the trade unions differed surprisingly little from those of previous governments. When, for example, the dockers and tramwaymen went on strike, they prepared to bring the Emergency Powers Act into force, an Act which they had bitterly opposed when it was passed. This was a clear and salutary lesson for the Labour movement. Obviously a Labour government, just like any other, had responsibilities towards the public at large which must over-rule its sympathies for any single pressure group. Similarly the trade unions had towards their members responsibilities which had to be discharged whatever government was in power. Although in the last resort the party and the unions depended on each other, their functions were different.

Ramsay MacDonald made matters worse by his unsympathetic attitude towards union matters. He scorned what he called 'the whirlpool of class-conscious trade unionists'. His cabinet of twenty included only seven union men, and during his term of office he spoke to the General Secretary of the TUC only once, for five minutes.

27 Red Friday

In 1924 Stanley Baldwin became Conservative Prime Minister for the second time. His two favourite boasts were 'I am not a clever man' and 'I am a man of peace', both of which were true. His modest appearance and moderate policies suited the mood of the time and earned him the trust and affection of the majority. But behind his calm exterior lay a dread of all things dramatic and demanding which made him nervous and indecisive in a crisis.

In July 1925 he had to face another conflict between capital and labour, with the coal industry once again at the centre. This crisis was partly of the government's own making. In April the value of the pound sterling as against other currencies had been raised. As a result British goods were priced out of foreign markets. The coal industry was particularly hard hit, especially as most pits were already running at a loss.

The mine-owners' answer was predictable — reduce prices by cutting miners' wages and increasing their working hours. Baldwin, though embarrassed by the 'stupid and discourteous' behaviour of the coal bosses, regretfully admitted that all workers would have to take cuts 'to help put industry on its feet'.

This naturally alarmed the unions. The TUC General Council decided they must support the miners, and informed the government that unless the coal-owners' lockout notices were withdrawn, a total ban on the transport of coal would begin on July 31st.

Baldwin averted the clash by granting a nine-month subsidy to prop up mining wages and profits, and appointing a Royal Commission of Inquiry under a Liberal lawyer, Sir Herbert Samuel.

The unions were jubilant at the government's surrender. Only a few leaders, including the miners, realised that they had only won a truce, not a victory. For the moment this was 'Red Friday', an atonement for that Black Friday of 1921. The whole movement basked in the warm glow of brotherly feeling.

The subsidy and the Samuel Commission provided a breathing place in which the problems of the coal industry could and should have been resolved. Baldwin and the General Council thankfully retired from the battle-ground and waited for Samuel's report, which they hoped would provide the basis of a negotiated settlement. But meanwhile extremists on both sides got to work.

The Cabinet itself was divided between moderates, led by Baldwin and Lord Birkenhead, and diehards led by Winston Churchill, Neville Chamberlain, and Joynson-Hicks the Home Secretary, who declared, 'The danger is not over. Sooner or later this question has got to be fought out. Is England to be governed by Parliament and the Cabinet or by a handful of trade union leaders?' In preparation for the fight, he laid detailed plans with special Emergency Local Committees and told them to stand by for a telegram from Whitehall bearing the

33 *Herbert Smith,
President of the Miners' Federation*

single word 'Action!' Meanwhile a group of prominent public men formed an 'Organisation for the Maintenance of Supplies' (OMS), which began to recruit volunteers for special duties.

Unfortunately the leadership of the Miners' Federation was in the hands of two obstinate class warriors. Herbert Smith, the President, had been born in a Yorkshire workhouse and grew up as an orphan. He had once been a prize-fighter and looked like it. His manner was blunt. At the negotiating table he was liable to take out his false teeth, wipe them on his handkerchief, replace them, and say 'Nowt doin'.

A. J. Cook, the General Secretary, a fervent left-wing Socialist, was a useless administrator, but a dangerously talented soap-box orator. Most of his time and energy was spent touring the coalfields, whipping up the miners' fury at open-air meetings. He coined their slogan: 'Not a penny off the pay, not a minute on the day'. He was spoiling for a fight on April 30th when the subsidy ran out. 'I don't care a hang for any government or army and navy', he boasted, 'they can come along with their bayonets. Bayonets don't cut coal.' He advised miners' families to lay up stocks of food for the battle. His own mother-in-law he said had been buying an extra tin of salmon a week. 'By God,' remarked J. H. Thomas sarcastically, 'A British revolution based on a tin of salmon!'

As for the coal-miners, they were ruthless enemies and unpopular allies. 'Not a prepossessing crowd', remarked Neville Chamberlain. Lord Birkenhead wrote that he'd thought the miners' leaders to be 'the stupidest men in England' – until he met the owners.

The Samuel Commission reported on March 6th. It ruled out nationalisation, but sternly recommended a complete re-organisation of the industry. It blamed the owners' selfishness and negligence for the bad labour relations, and suggested improvements. It supported the miners' demand for a national wage agreement. Although it opposed longer working hours, it judged that the miners would have to accept small and temporary wage-cuts.

The Report pleased neither party and the negotiations were a farce. The owners refused even to discuss it and stuck to their original demands. The Miners' Federation refused to discuss pay cuts unless all the

Report's recommendations were carried out immediately.

With only a fortnight to go before the threatened lockout, the government and the General Council tried in vain to bring the two sides to some compromise. But it was like standing between two colliding express trains. On April 30th the lockout began. The government immediately announced a State of Emergency, and the OMS assembled its volunteers. On the 31st, the General Council at last announced its plans for a General Strike to start at midnight on May 3rd. But even at this eleventh hour it battled desperately to avoid a showdown. At Downing Street members of the General Council and the Cabinet talked and talked. Meanwhile at the Memorial Hall, Farringdon Road, a special conference of 800 trade union delegates awaited news and instructions, whiling away the time by singing hymns and music-hall songs. On May 2nd agreement was in sight, but at the last minute Baldwin broke off negotiations when he heard that the *Daily Mail* typesetters had refused to print a violently anti-union article. The strike was on.

28 The General Strike

On the morning of Tuesday May 4th 1926, public transport all over the country came to a halt. J. R. Clynes recalled, 'The railway stations were silent and empty. In London only about 40 buses ran out of a total of 5,000. Underground stations were deserted. But throughout the day the streets were thronged with black crawling masses of pedestrians, cars, bicycles, horse vehicles — even people on roller skates.'

It was not yet a total strike. Only workers in selected industries were called out immediately: railways, road transport, docks, building, metal, power stations and printing. But this was quite enough completely to disrupt the normal life of the country. Both the General Council and the government were astonished by the enthusiastic response of the workers. Only a handful turned up for work. The majority were carried away by an exhilarating feeling of class solidarity and an unselfish sympathy for the miners. This was remarkable at a time of high unemployment when they ran the risk of losing their jobs and pensions. In addition to the million locked out miners, one and a half million men went on strike.

The General Council was ill-prepared for such a complete stoppage. Its central command was patchy and hesitant, and its communications with the regions inadequate. The day-to-day running of the strike therefore depended on a network of improvised local strike committees which generally showed unexpected initiative and efficiency.

The government's organisation was much more thorough. With the police, the army and navy, and thousands of volunteers at its command, it managed to restart the power stations and move essential food supplies. Moreover, thanks to the General Council's unwise decision to call out the newspaper printers, the government was left in control of the two main sources of information and propaganda, the BBC and the official *British Gazette*.

The *Gazette*, edited by the swashbuckling Mr Churchill, turned out to be rather an embarrassment. Churchill wanted the full force of the army turned onto the strikers, and wrote rousing editorials urging soldiers and volunteer constables to action. He branded the unions as 'the enemy' and demanded 'unconditional surrender'. Fortunately he was restrained by Baldwin and rebuked by George V, who were anxious not to enflame the strikers.

Over most of the country the strikers' behaviour was remarkably good-humoured and considerate. London busmen immobilised their buses by stripping the engines, but were careful to label all the parts for immediate reassembly after the strike. Builders working on hospitals carried on as usual. Strike pickets and policemen shared cups of tea and gossip, and even played friendly football matches together. The General Council and the local strike committees set the lead by advising the men to pretend they were on holiday. 'Keep smiling. Refuse to be provoked. Get into your garden. Look after the wife and kiddies.'

For many middle-class people too, the strike was an exciting change from normal routine – rather a lark. University undergraduates and medical students careered around in noisy sports cars delivering milk. They unloaded ships and drove buses plastered with stickers such as 'Don't throw stones at us; the passengers are in enough danger already!' Retired colonels and picturesque aristocrats joyfully drove, or tried to drive, railway trains. The strikers usually found the volunteers so comical, with their plus-fours, their beaming faces and their amateur incompetence, that they had not the heart seriously to molest them.

But in the poorer working-class areas, the strikers were often bitter and violent. There were ugly scenes in London's dockland when cargoes were unloaded by naval ratings under armed guard and carried through the streets in convoys flanked by armoured cars. In Glasgow there were frequent street fights between police and pickets, and several buses were overturned. There were similar incidents in other Northern cities. Miraculously, no one was killed. But each day that the strike dragged on increased the possibility of widespread violence and bloodshed.

No one was more conscious of this danger

34 & 35 *The two faces of the General strike (above) Cheerful volunteers, after passing their driving tests, at the London General Omnibus depot (below) Cargoes leaving the London docks under armed convoy.*

than the members of the General Council, who shuddered at the mere suggestion of revolution. Some of them dreaded victory almost more than defeat. Baldwin played on their fears by accusing them of a deliberate attack on the government and Parliament.

The Negotiating committee anxiously searched behind the scenes for a way out. On May 6th, Jimmy Thomas contacted Sir Herbert Samuel, who agreed to act as mediator. He drew up a list of proposals for a settlement more favourable to the miners than his Report. The General Council supported this Samuel Memorandum, but the miners, indignant at being kept in the dark, and enraged at further mention of wage-reductions, rejected it. Baldwin made vague gestures of goodwill, but refused to commit himself. Samuel hoped the government would co-operate, but as his position was unofficial, could not guarantee anything.

The General Council, still hesitating, called out its second line of strikers on May 11th, including the engineers and shipyard workers. But on May 12, after a last futile attempt to pacify the miners the negotiating committee told Baldwin that the General Council had decided to call off the strike.

It was a painful interview. Baldwin congratulated them on their wisdom, but refused to discuss Samuel's proposals for the mining industry, or the immediate future of the strikers. As he left Downing Street Bevin remarked, 'We have committed suicide. Thousands of members will be victimised as a result of this day's work.'

He was right. On May 13th, strikers reporting back to work were confronted by threats of the sack, loss of promotion and pensions, longer hours and pay cuts. They heard on the BBC Baldwin's triumphant claim of total victory. They learned to their disgust that the miners' dispute had not been settled. Bewildered and angry they went back on strike. By May 14th the number of strikers had actually increased by 10,000. They felt betrayed by the General Council, which in turn felt betrayed by the government. Fortunately after two days Baldwin reprimanded the employers for their vindictive conduct, and the majority of strikers were reinstated.

The miners stayed out for another six months but were eventually forced back to work on far harsher terms than those offered before the strike. Their wages were savagely cut and their hours lengthened. National bargaining was abandoned and settlements were imposed district by district. The Samuel Report's proposals for reorganisation were ignored. The British coal industry continued to decline, and hundreds of pits were closed. By 1928 one third of the miners were unemployed and over a million women and children were destitute. The Prince of Wales launched a National Appeal for money and cast-off clothing for victims of the industrial war. The Miners' Federation became more like a charity organisation than a union and never gained its old strength and importance.

For a time it seemed as if the trade-union movement would tear itself apart in bitter recriminations over the failure of the General Strike. The rank and file blamed the General Council and the General Council blamed the miners' leaders. Jimmy Thomas insisted that the General Council had saved the Labour movement from disunity and bankruptcy, and the country from bloodshed and chaos.

The government rubbed salt into labour's wounds by passing the Trades Disputes Act, which banned sympathetic strikes and 'strikes designed to coerce the government'. The Labour Party, unfairly blamed for encouraging the strike, was also punished. Instead of allowing objectors to 'contract out' of paying the political levy, the Act stated that all unionists wishing to contribute to party funds must 'contract in'. Many lukewarm supporters did not bother, and the party's income fell by more than a quarter. (The Act was repealed by the 1945 Labour government.)

So the General Strike, in spite of the enthusiasm and solidarity of the strikers, achieved nothing. Wages continued to fall and unemployment to rise. Union funds reached rock-bottom. Membership fell steadily because workers lost faith in the unions' ability to protect their living standards during an economic depression. The Communist Party gained many new recruits both among intellectuals and disillusioned trade unionists.

However, one effect of the strike was to clear the air of some of the stale myths of the class war. Many trade unionists had long believed in the general strike as the invincible weapon which one day would surely bring them victory. Now this belief had been shattered. Many employers had pretended for years that if they refused to recognise the existence of trade unions, the sensible British working man would eventually abandon them. The solidarity of the strikers had proved them wrong. Most employers, particularly the growing class of professional managers who were in many industries replacing the old-style capitalists, now realised that their interests would be better served by consulting the unions than by antagonising them.

Between 1927 and 1930 an important group of employers, led by Sir Alfred Mond, Chairman of Imperial Chemical Industries, held a series of informal discussions with various leaders of industrial problems. These 'Mond-Turner' talks helped to convince the unions that higher wages were more likely to come from increased production than from industrial warfare.

The result of these more reasonable and realistic attitudes on both sides can easily be shown by a few figures. In 1923 *three* out of *ten* strikes were caused by the refusal of employers to recognise or negotiate with unions; between 1927 and 1939 only *three* out of a *hundred*. Between 1918 and 1926 an average of 40 million working days were lost each year through industrial disputes;

between 1929 and 1939 only 3 million.

Admittedly this fall in the number of strikes was partly due to the unions' weakness. The failure of the General Strike had sapped their fighting spirit and their means to fight. The economic depression meant there was no extra money to fight for. Yet even after 1934 when trade perked up again and union membership began to recover, there was no return to the old battlefields.

29 The General Council under Citrine and Bevin

Never was the trade union movement more fortunate in its leaders than during the thirteen years between the General Strike and the Second World War. The power and authority of the General Council was steadily increased by two men of exceptional ability and energy — Walter Citrine and Ernest Bevin. Together they nursed the unions back to strength, restored their self-respect, and imposed new attitudes and policies. It was a remarkable partnership, considering the striking difference between their backgrounds and temperaments.

Unlike most union leaders of the past, Citrine had never been a slum kid, a soap-box orator or a militant strike-leader. He had spent his working life in the new and prosperous electrical industry, and had been General Secretary of the Electrical Trades Union. In 1926 at the age of thirty-nine he became

36 *Ernest Bevin and Walter Citrine 1937*

TUC General Secretary, a post he held until 1946.

His qualities and talents were those of the perfect civil servant. He was an expert negotiator, an efficient administrator, a calm and lucid public speaker. At the TUC he provided the facts and Bevin the fireworks.

Ernest Bevin, the son of a Somerset farm-worker, was orphaned at six and started work at eleven. As a young man he was a van-driver and local union leader in Bristol. In 1920 he became Assistant General Secretary of the Dockers' Union, and because of his natural eloquence was chosen to present the Dockers' case to the Shaw Tribunal on pay and conditions.

He spoke almost non-stop for three days, listing the injustices and hardships suffered by the dockers, laying bare the facts, interrogating the employers. His command of detail was highly effective. He proved, for example, that a docker hauled more weight in a day than a dockside carthorse in a week. And the horses were better fed! The employers claimed that £3 12s. 6d. a week was enough for a family to live on. This made Bevin so indignant that he bought £3 12s. 6d worth of food in the market, divided it into five, thrust the meagre portions at the employers' witnesses, and asked whether they could do heavy manual work on such a diet. Their obvious embarrassment proved his point.

The Tribunal's award was favourable to the dockers. Bevin won high praise from the judge, not only for his presentation of the facts, but for his impassioned appeal on behalf of 'those who toil' for the right to 'mastery of their own lives'. From his fellow-unionists he earned the honorary legal title of 'The dockers' KC'.

This experience coloured Bevin's future attitude to industrial disputes. Though never afraid of strike action if there seemed no alternative, he saw it as a last resort. 'Cannot we fight by discussion as well as starvation?' he asked, 'Cannot we fight by intelligence?' All through his career he tried to educate himself and his fellow-unionists away from a narrow concern for their own immediate interests a wider understanding of politics and economics. In 1929 he pushed the unions along this path by setting up the important TUC Economic Committee. He also rescued the ailing *Daily Herald*, which besides being a useful mouthpiece for the Labour Movement, became a very popular newspaper – the first to reach a daily circulation of 2 million.

In spite of all his other activities, Bevin kept a firm grip on the TGWU. Against a background of bad trade and rising unemployment all he could do was try to limit wage-reductions and preserve national agreements against better days. Such a defensive policy was naturally unpopular, and the TGWU, like other unions, lost many members. Disgruntled militants among the dockers and London bus-drivers whipped up unofficial strikes, and held rowdy meetings where Bevin was often insulted and sometimes physically assaulted. His toughness on such occasions gave him a reputation among his enemies as something of a bully, but it held the union together at a difficult time.

In 1928 Ramsay MacDonald performed the opening ceremony at Transport House, the TGWU's huge office block in Westminster. As a gesture of goodwill Bevin had invited the TUC and the Labour Party to share the building, which became, and remains to this day, the centre of the Labour Movement. Unfortunately this symbol of unity could not conceal the divisions between the unions and the party, or between Bevin and MacDonald.

The second Labour Government of 1929–31 was an even more bitter experience for the unions than the first. Once again they watched a weak minority government floundering helplessly in a bog of stagnant trade and chronic unemployment. The root cause of the trouble was a financial crisis in America which upset world trade and caused terrible hardship throughout Europe. The government could hardly be blamed for that. But it was too timid and unimaginative to try any new remedies, even when the number of unemployed rose to $2\frac{3}{4}$ millions in July 1931. MacDonald, J. H. Thomas and Philip Snowden the Chancellor, on the advice of the Conservative opposition and the bankers, decided that the only solution was a sharp cut in government spending, including the dole.

The General Council, particularly Bevin, thought that this would be self-defeating. They believed that the economy was rotting because people were spending too little, not too much, and that to make the poor poorer was unwise as well as unjust. Unemployment could be reduced, they insisted, by raising the school leaving-age, making retirement at sixty-five compulsory, and by providing jobs in state-financed industries. These proposals were brushed aside.

In August 1931 MacDonald resigned because a majority of his cabinet refused to agree to cutting the dole and forming a National Government in alliance with the Conservatives and Liberals. Only a handful of Labour ministers and members followed MacDonald; the majority went into opposition. McDonald was branded as a traitor and expelled from the party.

In the following general election, Labour lost 243 seats and held only 49. Many important figures, including the leader Arthur Henderson, were defeated. People voted Nationalist because it seemed the patriotic thing to do in face of the financial crisis. In fact the government was Conservative in all but name. In 1935 Baldwin succeeded MacDonald as Prime Minister.

The Trade Union Movement did great service to the shattered Labour Party in those dismal years. It provided money, support and above all leadership. Its efforts were rewarded in the election of 1935 when Labour increased its representation to 154.

Under a wise and moderate new leader, Clement Atlee, Labour became a strong and respected Opposition.

Bevin became the key man in Labour politics. He fought tirelessly against the extreme left wing, which was trying to pull the party towards the Communists. Like most trade-union leaders he was a practical man, and he thought the ideas of middle-class intellectuals like Stafford Cripps were highly dangerous. He persuaded the party to reject their all-or-nothing Socialism, and adopt a programme of moderate reform. He also won an important victory in foreign policy over the large pacifist group in the party which opposed all 'capitalist' wars. He realised earlier than most politicians of any party the danger of another war with Germany. His contacts with German trade unionists, who were being brutally persecuted by the Nazis, convinced him that Hitler must be defeated by force. It was largely due to his eloquence that Labour eventually accepted the need for re-armament.

A similar battle was fought within the Conservative Party between the government of Mr Chamberlain, which hoped to come to terms with Germany, and a belligerent group led by Winston Churchill. For once Bevin and that old arch-enemy of Labour spoke with one voice.

30 The Second World War

In May 1940, nine months after Britain's declaration of war on Germany, the military situation in Europe was desperate. Britain seemed to be on the brink of defeat. The faltering Mr Chamberlain was replaced as Prime Minister by Winston Churchill who immediately invited the Opposition to join his Coalition Government. Mr Atlee became deputy Prime Minister, and several other Labour men were given important ministries. The most significant appointment was that of Ernest Bevin as Minister of Labour. It brought the trade unions right into the heart of the government to an extent never considered in the previous war.

This was a war between highly industrial nations, which would be decided as much by the capacity of each side to produce tanks, aircraft, bombs and other weapons as by the courage of their armies. Industry had to be completely reorganised, and the workers mobilised and directed as efficiently as the troops: an immense task which could only be achieved with the active help of the unions. Bevin, the most powerful and forceful union leader, was the obvious man for the job.

37 *VE Day, 8 May 1945: King George VI at Buckingham Palace with Churchill, Bevin and other members of the Coalition Government*

He was given overall command of the supply of manpower for industry and the armed forces, with unprecedented power over the lives and activities of civilians. He could order anyone to go anywhere and do any job he considered necessary. Skilled workers in essential industries were forbidden to change jobs without permission from his ministry. The employers' right to hire and dismiss workers was equally strictly controlled. Women were conscripted for war work. Unskilled workers were trained to take over skilled jobs. Thousands of unemployed men were set to work.

Strikes and lockouts were declared illegal. Disputes which could not be settled through normal collective bargaining were sent to a National Arbitration Tribunal. Unofficial strike leaders could be fined or imprisoned. Union rules and restrictions on such matters as overtime and the allocation of jobs between different grades of skill were suspended. But instead of having to make sacrifices and submit unquestioningly to orders from above as in 1914, the unions shared in the direction of the war effort.

At every stage and at every level from the TUC downwards, they were consulted. Citrine recalls, 'I had interviews galore with Ministers and their top civil servants. I almost wore out the doormats in Whitehall.' At the top was a joint Consultative Committee composed of seven trade-union and seven employers' representatives, set up to advise Bevin on a vast range of problems, including conscription, the allocation of labour and food-rationing. A similar committee dealt with arms production. These were backed up by a network of Joint Committees at regional and workshop level, which were responsible for putting government policies into action.

During the 1914–18 war co-operation between unions, employers and the government often led to bitterness and rebellion among the rank and file. But during the Second World War, although co-operation was far closer, there were hardly any unofficial strikes. The Communist shop stewards, who had frequently disrupted industry during the previous war, were totally committed to the fight against Fascism, especially after Hitler's invasion of Russia in 1941, and worked strenuously towards increasing arms production. The working class felt far more urgently involved in this war. Fear of invasion, hatred of Hitler, and German bombing raids on British cities –

the Blitz – united the entire British population in a way it had never been before.

In the interests of efficiency and national morale, the government followed a policy of 'war socialism'. Essential industries were placed under state control. Industrial production was planned down to the smallest detail, wasteful luxuries were cut out. Food prices were held steady. The workers' welfare was carefully catered for. Factory canteens were opened and men doing heavy manual work were given extra rations. The workers did not feel, as they had in the First World War, that they were bearing an unfair burden of hardship and sacrifice. Everyone was expected to obey orders, from dukes to dustmen. The rationing of food, clothes and fuel was the same for everybody. Taxes on the salaries, profits and dividends of the well-to-do were raised to levels that would previously have been considered intolerable. Manufacturers of war supplies were prevented from making unfair profits. Meanwhile wages were generously increased, especially for the low-paid workers like miners and agricultural labourers. These measures brought about a dramatic levelling of wealth, and encouraged trade unionists to respond willingly to the demands made upon them.

The war brought many changes which the trade unions had long worked for; strong government control over industry, the extension of collective wage-bargaining, improvements in social welfare, greater equality of wealth, and above all full employment. These were all part of the Labour Party's plan for post-war Britain. In 1944, with the end of the war in sight, it published a manifesto called *'Let us face the future'*, which was fully supported by the TUC. It promised that a Labour government would increase and extend social-security benefits such as sickness and unemployment pay, old-age pensions and child allowances, and introduce a National Health Service to provide free medical care. Britain would become a Welfare State in which citizens would be insured against want literally 'from the cradle to the grave'. It also committed a Labour government to the nationalisation of key industries and to a policy of full employment.

In July 1945, two months after the end of the war with Germany, the Coalition split up and there was a general election. The Conservatives, confident that Churchill's immense popularity would carry the day, offered no clear programme to the voters. Instead they thundered about the virtues of free enterprise and the horrors of Socialism. But the voters had not forgotten the mass unemployment that had accompanied Conservative free enterprise before the war. Most of them had willingly swallowed a large dose of Socialism during the last five years, and had been impressed by the conduct of the trade unions and the Labour Party. Churchill was indeed a hero, but so was Ernie Bevin in his way.

The election resulted in a massive victory for Labour, with an overall majority of nearly 150. For the first time a Labour government had the power and the popular support to carry out Socialist policies which had long been demanded by the unions.

31 The search for a wages policy

The close links forged between government and unions during the war have never since been broken, although at times they have been severely strained. They have survived the change from Labour to Conservative in 1951, and back to Labour again in 1964. The General Council is consulted regularly on industrial and economic matters, whichever party is in power.

To their surprise and sorrow, the unions have discovered that Labour governments are not necessarily easier to deal with than Conservative governments. They are bound to the Labour Party by shared history and ideals, and by a network of personal and political friendships. They naturally expect more from a Labour government, and if their expectations are not fulfilled, they are correspondingly more bitter. When a Conservative government attacks their interests, they can say that the bosses are up to their usual wicked tricks. But when a Labour government attacks their interests, they feel that they have been betrayed by their friends. One constant and bitter cause of conflict has been wages policy.

Right from the start Mr Atlee's government made repeated appeals to its trade union allies to moderate wage demands. The war had left Britain almost bankrupt. The standard of living could only be maintained, let alone improved, by a gigantic effort to increase exports. If wages were allowed to rise too quickly, British goods would become too expensive to compete in overseas markets. The ambitious programme of reforms to which the government and the unions were committed had to be paid for. Millions of pounds were needed to launch the new nationalised industries. Millions more would have to be invested in the Welfare State. It was not enough to 'soak the rich' – they were already taxed up to the hilt. The workers would have to pay their share.

The government's call for wage restraint put the union leaders in a painfully embarrassing situation. Since 1945 they had become very much part of the ruling order. Several prominent unionists had been made members of the government. Others had been promoted to the Boards of nationalised industries, or given peerages or knighthoods, in reward for loyalty past, present, and future. The rank and file were already apprehensive about too close an identification between their leaders and the government. An official pact to limit wages would only confirm their suspicions.

Nevertheless, the General Council reluctantly decided in 1948 to co-operate with the government's campaign for voluntary wage restraint. At a time of full employment, with employers bidding against each other for labour, this was easier said than done. But for two years wages were held in check, in spite of the practical and political difficulties. By 1950 the economic situation had improved, and the TUC voted overwhelmingly against further restraint. Many trade unionists were so sour about the austerity of the past six years that they voted Conservative in the 1951 election.

For the first four years of Conservative rule, relations between the unions and the government were fairly cordial. But in 1955 the united and moderate leadership of the General Council broke up, and Frank Cousins, the militant new General Secretary of the TGWU became the dominant figure. The number of strikes greatly increased, and the public placed most of the blame on the unions. In 1959 George Woodcock, the new General Secretary of the TUC, admitted that the unions were more unpopular than they had ever been, and had 'lost the general sympathy which the public usually reserves for the underdog.' The Labour Party, already weak and divided, suffered further from the unpopularity of the unions, and in the general elections of 1955 and 1959, the Conservatives increased their majority. As many as three in ten trade unionists voted Conservative. They agreed with Prime Minister Harold Macmillan's famous boast – 'You've never had it so good!'

Until 1960 annual wage increases had come to be taken almost for granted. But it was becoming obvious that this apparent prosperity was only skin-deep. Ever since the war the British had been habitually paying themselves (in wages and imports) more than they had earned (in production and exports). Several times the Conservative government had tried to clamp down on wage increases, but union pressure had proved too strong. In 1961, during a serious financial crisis, the government tried to impose a 'wage freeze', but its resolution soon crumbled under a fierce assault from the unions.

In 1962 the seriousness of the economic situation and the size of Britain's debts to foreign countries converted the Conservatives to the need for long-term economic planning. The government was particularly anxious about the low level of 'productivity' – the amount produced by workers and machines in a given time. It began to search for a fair and workable incomes policy which would make increases in wages dependent on high productivity. As a first step the government decided to form a new top-level planning organisation, the National Economic Development Council, commonly known as Neddy. Its job would be to examine the long-term industrial prospects and provide the government with plans and forecasts to guide its economic policies. The government was anxious to secure the goodwill and expert knowledge of the unions, as well as employers and economists. Many unionists were hostile because they suspected that Neddy might be used as a device for controlling wages. But the General Council decided to accept the challenge, in the hope that it would bring 'a greater share in decisions about the industries in which our members work, and more influence over national economic and social policies which affect our members as workers and citizens.'

In 1964 Labour was once again returned to power. The Prime Minister Harold Wilson promised to 'get Britain moving again' after thirteen years of 'stop-go'. Higher production would be rewarded by higher wages. But the government soon discovered that the economic situation was far worse than it had expected. The bold forecasts and encouraging promises of election year gave way to familiar appeals for restraint, discipline, and extra effort. The public was told that Britain's future prosperity depended on the enforcement of a Prices and Incomes Policy far more severe than had ever been attempted before.

The broad aims of the policy were, and still are: to limit increases in incomes to a level the country can afford, and to reduce the demand for higher incomes by holding prices down. As far as the unions are concerned, this means that they can only expect wage increases if their members are particularly badly paid, or if they can offer higher productivity in return, by surrendering restrictive practices, and generally co-operating with any changes management wishes to make.

Although most responsible people now recognise that some sort of Prices and Incomes Policy is fair and necessary, it has proved extremely difficult to put into practice. Any manufacturer can always think of a good reason for raising his prices, just as any trade union leader can always justify a wage claim. At first the government tried to get the employers and unions to co-operate voluntarily in the control of prices, dividends and wages. It set up a Prices and Incomes Board to assess the merits of claims for higher prices or wages. But, as so often in the past, voluntary methods had little affect. In July 1966, during yet another financial crisis, the government ordered a six month freeze on wages and dividends, followed by an indefinite period of severe restraint. Under the Prices and Incomes Act it became compulsory to notify the government of proposed increases in wages or prices, on pain of fine, or even imprisonment.

These measures enraged the unions. Any extension of the law, particularly any attempt to impose legal penalties, always does enrage the unions. The Prices and Incomes Act was regarded as a brutal attack on the sacred principle of free collective bargaining, and upon the General Council's own efforts to control wage claims. Unions leaders who had at first agreed with the policy soon became woefully disillusioned, while those who had always opposed it did all they could to sabotage it. Frank Cousins, whom Mr Wilson had hoped to tame by making Minister of Technology, resigned from the Cabinet to lead his union into the attack. At the TUC the majority vote against the government grew larger each year. To make matters worse, unemployment rose after 1966 to the highest level since 1940. This painful fact made it almost impossible for even the most loyal union leaders to defend the government's policies.

32 The need for reform

The British trade union movement is rightly proud of being the oldest in the world. Its struggle against the harshness and inhumanity of nineteenth-century industrialism, and its passionate involvement in the democratic cause, form one of the noblest chapters in our history. But ever since the unions obtained the power they had fought for, they have become embarrassingly old-fashioned. In the immediate post-war period they rested on their laurels and did little to adapt their organisations to the changing pattern of industry. The TUC itself grew somewhat conservative and complacent. The best cartoonist of the period David Low, always portrayed it as a lumbering carthorse, sturdy and reliable, but sadly out of date.

From 1959 to 1969 the TUC had as General Secretary a dedicated reformer, George Woodcock, but his appeals for change had little practical effect. He soon learnt the truth of Bevin's remark, 'The most conservative

38 *George Woodcock, General Secretary of the TUC, 1959–69, and his successor Victor Feather, singing* Auld Lang Syne *at the end of the 1968 Trade Union Congress.*

man in the world is the British trade unionists when you want to change him.' It took Bevin ten years to persuade fourteen transport unions to merge into the giant TGWU. Even then he might well have failed but for the pressure of economic depression. During periods of prosperity and full employment, it has proved almost impossible to persuade unions with long histories and proud traditions to surrender their separate identities. Unlike other countries where trade unionism is newer and more flexible, such as the USA, Britain has few unions which represent all the workers in a single industry. The National Union of Mineworkers is the only large industrial union. Even in modern industries like chemicals and aircraft, several unions overlap and compete. The time and temper wasted on inter-union rivalry is appalling.

The trouble stems from the traditional predominance of the craft unions. The survival of tiny unions like The Amalgamated Union of Sailmakers (75 members) and The Sheffield Sawgrinders Protection Society (346 members) is charming and probably harmless. But in some cases the survival of craft unions or of craft traditions within large unions has had a disastrous effect on industrial relations. The printing industry is cruelly handicapped by the number and variety of specialised unions which still exist. So is the steel industry, which has eighteen unions, as against one in West Germany. The railways have long suffered from the rivalry between the NUR and ASLEF. Motor manufacturers have to deal with innumerable competing unions, including some like the Vehicle Builders which date back to the days of the stage-coach. And in ship-building, although the various craft unions have amalgamated, traditional demarcation rules which belong to the age of wooden sailing ships are still observed.

As a result, these industries employ up to 30 per cent more people than they need, are torn by inter-union disputes, and crippled by restrictive practices. The printing unions are particularly adept at keeping alive irrelevant craft practices. They often refuse to work new machines; they insist on long apprenticeships which could be completed in half the time; they even sometimes insist on the employment of craftsmen to sweep the floor in newspaper composing rooms.

On the railways many of the skills and responsibilities which ASLEF represents are now obsolete. Each year large numbers of ASLEF men become redundant and lose their jobs. More and more traditionally ASLEF jobs are being filled with NUR men. Yet ASLEF refuses to die. Instead it fights for lost causes, insisting for example that every train should carry a guard even when there is no guard's van. The union was formed in the days of steam-trains, and has yet to come to terms with diesel and electric trains.

In the shipyards the union rule-book is followed with almost comic solemnity. The job of making a port-hole, it states, requires a joiner, a shipwright, a driller, a burner, a welder and a caulker. While each man does his special task, the others just stand around watching. The unions know that two men working continuously could do the job in a fraction of the time and at a fraction of the cost. It also knows that large numbers of craftsmen's mates have little work to do. But it fears that if it relaxes the rules, many men will become redundant.

Shipbuilding and the railways are declining industries. The fear of unemployment is certainly understandable and restrictive practices (the unions prefer to call them 'protective' practices) might be justifiable. But ultimately they work against the unions' own interests. The railways already run at a heavy loss; once modernised, and unburdened by surplus manpower, they could afford to pay higher wages. The poor reputation of British shipyards has lost them a lot of custom to more efficient rivals such as the Japanese. Some have even been forced to close, adding to the numbers of unemployed in already depressed areas. A full order-book provides far better security of employment than any number of protective practices.

Detailed co-operation between unions and management is commonplace in some other countries, notably in Sweden, but it is still comparatively rare in Britain. Most British unions still cling to their traditional distrust of capitalism and the boss class. Except among a few progressive white-collar unions, there is a distaste for 'business unionism' such as exists in the USA and Germany, and a fear that sitting round glossy boardroom tables with company directors, or investing union funds in stocks and shares, might tame and corrupt their working-class souls. Even if they could overcome these inhibitions, it is doubtful whether their organisations would be equipped for the extra responsibilities that industrial partnership would involve.

In many ways the majority of unions resemble well-intentioned but ramshackle welfare organisations, with their cumbersome constitutions, their shabby under-staffed offices, their reluctance to employ outside experts such as accountants, and their indifference to public relations. Efficient modern charities like Oxfam put them to shame. The way they treat their officials is extraordinarily tight-fisted. Even the general secretaries and presidents of huge manual unions rarely get much over £2,000 a year. Yet these are men who spend most of their time and energy extracting as much money as possible from the employers for their members; men who wield more power than any managing director they might confront across the bargaining table.

Lowlier officials are often worse off than many of the men they represent, in spite of the long hours and worrying responsibilities their jobs involve. It is hardly surprising that there is now a serious shortage of full-time

39 *London dockers vote for an overtime ban, on 12 August 1965. In the foreground, Jack Dash, the well-known Communist unofficial leader*

officials. Most unions rely on large numbers of unpaid volunteers both in the branch offices and on the factory floor. Inevitably the men who are willing to take on these harassing jobs tend to be militant, and quite a number are Communists. But the majority are responsible hard-working men. It is a tribute to our trade-union traditions that there are so few cases of corruption. (In America union officers frequently take bribes and run all sorts of frauds and fiddles and sometimes behave more like gangsters than workers' representatives.)

For most members, the shop steward on the factory floor is their only contact with the union. On average, only 5 per cent regularly attend branch meetings. The percentage voting in union elections, even for the top posts, is little higher. The whole regional and branch structure of many unions is in a state of decay. Communication between the union leadership and their rank and file is virtually nil. The official procedure for settling disputes is painfully slow and rigid. This makes it all too easy for local firebrands to persuade their frustrated workmates to take the law into their own hands. *95 per cent of all strikes in Britain are unofficial.* The strikers often do not even bother to inform their unions.

We have been so obsessed by strikes recently that it is not generally realised that Britain's strike record is only about average for a leading industrial nation. In fact it is far better than that of the USA. Many more working days are lost each year through sickness, accidents and absenteeism (people giving themselves the day off) than through strikes. Bad management and restrictive practices do just as much damage to the economy as strikes. But strikes get more publicity; they cause more inconvenience and arouse greater indignation. Many unofficial strikes seem quite pointless and unforgivably selfish. Although only small groups are directly involved, thousands of innocent workers suffer from the disruption that 'wild-cat' strikes cause, particularly in the motor-car industry. They do at least as much damage to the economy as the comparatively rare large official strikes and they undermine trade-union democracy. When the executive of a union calls a strike, it acts on behalf of all its members. But 'wild-cat' strikers rarely see beyond their own particular grievance.

There is a growing demand, especially from Conservative politicians, for changes in the law governing trade unions in general and strikes in particular. The present laws were designed to protect the workers from oppression. They give British unions greater freedom and power than any other unions in the industrial world. Perhaps the time has now come to protect employers and consumers from the unions.

In 1966 the government set up a Royal Commission on Trade Unions and Employers' Associations under Lord Donovan to study industrial relations and suggest improvements. The Donovan Report, published in June 1968, advised against imposing legal penalties on strikers. Its conclusion was that fines, or worse still imprisonment, would be impossible to enforce, and would only make martyrs out of the men involved. Besides, it would be pointless and unjust to penalise anyone for breaking wage-agreements at the moment because collective bargaining is in such a state of chaos. Wage agreements must be simplified first, and then perhaps they could be enforced by law.

In most industries the weekly pay-packet consists of a basic wage plus extras — overtime and piecework payments, bonuses and incentive payments, and other factory or company additions to the minimum. The gap between basic wages and actual earnings is now so wide and so various that formal national bargaining between union leaders and employers' associations is becoming a hollow ritual. The Donovan Report suggests that national agreements should gradually be dropped in favour of factory or company agreements: not vague informal agreements, but detailed written agreements binding on both parties. They should cover not only wages, but also discipline, redundancy, pensions and other such matters, and be registered with a new Commission for Industrial Relations.

Donovan's diagnosis of our industrial ills has been widely accepted, but many people find the remedies proposed too gradual. The employers and the Conservatives would like to make all wage agreements legally binding on both parties, with penalties for breaking them. The Labour government was never prepared to go as far as that, but its Industrial Relations Bill, published in January 1969, was far more ambitious than had been expected.

It proposed the setting-up of a Commission for Industrial Relations as suggested in the Donovan Report. This body would be a friend to the unions rather than a foe. It would protect union members from unfair dismissal by their employers, and from unfair treatment by their unions. It would provide money for unions wishing to amalgamate or otherwise improve their organisations. It would try to prevent disputes by promoting improvements in collective bargaining procedures, and to settle them by persuasion. At its head would be George Woodcock himself, a man who has devoted his life to the reform of industrial relations by voluntary means.

The unions could hardly object to these

positive proposals, but they were horrified to discover that the government intended to go beyond Donovan's recommendations, and pass new laws to curb strikes. Unions could be ordered to hold a ballot of their members before calling an official strike. A compulsory 'conciliation pause' could be imposed during an unofficial strike to provide time to work out a settlement. During the pause the strikers would have to return to work, and the employers would have to suspend the innovations which had caused the strike. Anyone who defied the pause would be fined.

As in the Prices and Incomes Act, the very mention of penal clauses, the slightest possibility of trade unionists being fined or imprisoned, roused the unions to fever pitch. Throughout the spring of 1969 the government and the General Council argued furiously. The government insisted that the unions had shown themselves incapable and unwilling to deal with unofficial strikes, and that the time had come for the law to step in. The unions insisted that anti-strike laws would destroy the voluntary tradition of British industrial relations, and would prove unworkable and unfair. If the government went ahead with these laws, it could not expect the unions to deal with the industrial disruption they would cause. Nor could it expect the unions to continue providing the bulk of the Labour Party's funds.

Eventually the TUC offered the government an alternative. If the laws were dropped, it promised to assume new powers to intervene in unofficial strikes, and devise new penalties against unofficial strikers. Both the TUC and its member unions would tighten their discipline, and troublemakers would be dealt with swiftly and strictly. In June 1969, the government, alarmed by the hysteria of the Labour Movement, decided to drop its anti-strike proposals, and give the TUC one more chance.

Was the government's decision an abject surrender to union bullying, or a triumph for common-sense? Will the TUC's resolution prove strong enough, and its organisation efficient enough for the task it has taken upon itself? Has the Labour Movement been saved from self-destruction? These are questions which must soon be answered. The immediate future is uncertain and perilous. One thing though, is sure. If industrial relations do not improve, some future government is bound to try stronger medicine. This is probably the unions' last chance to work their own cure.

A select booklist

General Histories

G. D. H. COLE. *Short History of the British Working-class Movement.* Allen & Unwin, 1948 (Detailed and scholarly; contains many useful tables.)

G. D. H. COLE & R. POSTGATE. *The Common People.* Methuen, University Paperbacks, 1964 (A good social history, which sets the trade unions in a wider context. Useful bibliography.)

W. H. COURT. *A Concise Economic History of Britain.* Cambridge University Paperback, 1964 (A useful reference book, especially on distribution of taxes, the Poor Laws, the Factory Acts, and comparative incomes. Excellent chapters on the unions.)

G. PATTINSON. *An Outline of Trade Union History.* Barrie & Rocliff, 1962 (An introduction for young people.)

HENRY PELLING. *A History of British Trade Unionism.* Pelican Original, 1963 (Brief, but authoritative and up-to-date. Somewhat pedestrian in style. Contains a valuable and comprehensive bibliography, lists the most important primary sources and documents.)

FRANCIS WILLIAMS. *Magnificent Journey.* Odhams, 1954 (A lively account in the journalistic manner. Suitable for older schoolchildren.)

Special Periods

A. ASPINALL. *Early English Trade Unions.* Batchworth Press, 1949 (A collection of documents, with a valuable introduction and commentary.)

ASA BRIGGS. *Victorian People.* Odhams, 1954 (The chapter on Robert Applegarth of the carpenters' union.)

G. DANGERFIELD. *The Strange Death of Liberal England.* Capricorn Paperback, New York, 1961 (A fascinating account of the upheaval of 1910–14.)

C. L. MOWAT. *Britain Between the Wars.* Methuen, 1955 (A useful social history, with interesting accounts of the General Strike, unemployment, and the state of the mining industry.)

E. ROYSTON PIKE. *Human Documents of the Industrial Revolution.* Allen & Unwin, 1966 (A useful anthology.)

MICHAEL SHANKS. *The Stagnant Society.* Pelican, 1961 (The chapters on the present-day situation of the unions provide an excellent starting-point for classes.)

JULIAN SYMONS. *The General Strike.* Cresset Press, 1957

E. P. THOMPSON. *The Making of the English Working Class.* Gollancz, 1963 (An excellent and detailed account of the origins of working-class culture, with useful comment on religious influences, education, radical clubs, living standards, etc. Especially illuminating on the impact of the Industrial Revolution on the lives of working people.)

Report of the Royal Commission on Trade Unions and Employers' Associations, HMSO, 1965–8

Biography

A. BULLOCK. *The Life and Times of Ernest Bevin.* 2 volumes, Heinemann, 1960 (A fine portrait of perhaps the greatest of all union leaders, and a valuable and detailed account of the period 1900–50.)

Autobiography

WILL THORNE. *My Life's Battles*

BEN TILLET. *Memories and Reflections*

JOSEPH ARCH. *Autobiography*
(All difficult to obtain but should be available from libraries.)

Film
WHAT ABOUT THE WORKERS? *Available from:*
RANK Audio Visual Ltd, Rank Film Library, PO Box 70, Great West Road, Brentford, Middlesex.
(A factual compilation of contemporary prints, photographs and newsreel, covering the period 1889 to the present day.)

Index

(*References in italics are to illustrations*)

A
Allan, William, 23
Amalgamated Association of Miners, 33
Amalgamated Engineering Union (AEU), 23, 66
Amalgamated Society of Carpenters and Joiners, 25
Amalgamated Society of Engineers (ASE), 23-4, 25, 32, 37, 40, 58
Amalgamated Society of Railway Servants, 45, 47
Applegarth, Robert, 25, 26, 27
Arch, Robert, 34, 35, 36, *35*
Askwith, George, 51
ASLEF, 62, 86
Asquith, 47, 53, 57
Attlee, Clement, 66, 79, 82
Ayrshire Miners Union, 43

B
Baldwin, Stanley, 61, 69, 71, 72, 74, 78
Balfour, Arthur, 46
BBC, 72, 74
Beesley, Amman, 45
Belgium, invasion of, 57
Besant, Annie, 38
Bevin, Ernest, 66, 74, 76, 77, 78, 79, 80, 81, 85, 86, *76*, *80*
Birkenhead, Lord, 69, 70
'Black Friday', 63, 66, 69
'blackleg', 11
'blacklist', 11
Blackpool, Stephen, 27

Boer War, 41
Boilermakers' Society, 28, 41
Booth, Charles, 41, 43
Breeches-makers' Society, 13
British Gazette, 72
Broadhurst, Henry, 31, 33
Bryant & May, *see* match-girls' strike
Burns, John, 37, 38, 39, 40
Burt, Thomas, 30, 31

C
Campbell-Bannerman, Sir Henry, 46-7
Chamberlain, Neville, 69, 70, 79
Chatsworth House, 6
checkweighmen, 34
Churchill, Winston, 43, 50, 69, 72, 79, 81, *80*
Citrine, Walter, 76, 77, 80, *76*
Clynes, J. R., 64, 67, 71, *68*
Coal Mines Regulation Act (1872), 34
Combination Acts, 9-11, 13, 18-9, 28
Commission for Industrial Relations, 89-90
Communist Party of Great Britain, 67
Connelly, James, 54
Cook, A. J., 70
Cousins, Frank, 83, 85
Criminal Law Amendment Act (1871), 29, 30
Cripps, Stafford, 79

D
Daily Citizen, 55
Daily Herald, 55, 77
Daily Mail, 71
Dash, Jack, *88*
demarcation disputes, 33, 86
Devonport, Lord, 54

Devonshire, Duke of, 6
Dickens, Charles, 27
Disraeli, 30
Dock Wharf Riverside & General Labourers' Union, 40
'dole', 64, 78
Donovan, Lord, 89; Donovan Report, 89-90

E
Electrical Trades Union (ETU), 76
Emergency Powers Act (1920), 62, 68
Employers and Workmen Act (1875), 30

F
Fabian Society, 44
Factory Acts, 21, 22
Feather, Victor, *85*
French Revolution, 9
Friendly Society of Agricultural Labourers, 19

G
Game Laws, 19
Gasworkers and General Labourers Union, 38
Gaitskell, Hugh, 66
General Strike (1926), 60, 71-6
George III, 9, *10*
George V, 67, 72
George VI, *80*
Grand National Consolidated Trade Union, 18-9, 21
Grand Union of Operative Spinners, 18
Great Depression (1876-88), 31-2, 48
Great Exhibition (1851), 23

H
Hamilton, Lord Claude, 62
Hardie, James Keir, 43-4, *43*
Hebergram, Joseph, 16
Henderson, Arthur, 57, 67, 78
Hitler, 79, 80
Hodges, Frank, 63
Hornby v Close, 28
Housing Act (1924), 67
Hunger Marches, 64

I
Independent Labour Party (ILP), 43, 44
Industrial Courts, 60
Industrial Relations Bill, 89
Irish Transport Workers Federation (ITWF), 54-5
Iron and Steel Association, 66

J
Jolly George, 60
Joynson-Hicks, 69

K
Knight, Robert, 41

L
Labour Party, 44, 46-8, 55, 57, 67, 75, 78, 81-3
Labour Representation Committee (LRC), 44, 45, 46
laissez-faire, 9
Larkin, Jim, 54, 55
Lib/Labs, 31, 40, 43, 46
Lloyd George, 46, 47, 52, 57, 59, 61-2

Londonderry, Marquess of, 33
London Trades Council (LTC), 25-6
Loveless, George and John, 19
Ludd, General Ned, 12
Luddites, 12

M
Macdonald, Alexander, 30, 31, 33
Macdonald, Ramsay, 47, 48, 67, 68, 78, *68*
Macmillan, Harold, 83
Macready, General, 50
Manchester, factory conditions in, 15
Manchester Old Mechanics, 23
Manchester Trades Council, 30
Mann, Tom, 37, 38-9, 49-51, 56, *49*
Manning, Cardinal, 40
Marx, Karl, 37
Masters and Servants Act, 30
match-girls' strike, 37, *37*
Miners Federation of Great Britain, 40, 53, 55, 61, 62, 66, 70, 74
Miners' Minimum Wage Act (1912), 53
Mines Act (1847), 22
Mond, Sir Alfred, 75
'Mond-Turner Talks', 75

N
Napoleon, 11
National Agricultural Labourers Union, 36
National Arbitration Tribunal, 80
National Association for the Protection of Labour, 18
National Economic Development Council (NEDDY), 83-4
National Health Service, 81

National Insurance Act (1911), 46
National Miners' Union, 30, 33
National Union of General & Municipal Workers, 66
National Union of Mineworkers, 86
National Union of Railwaymen (NUR), 50, 55, 62, 86
New Lanark, 17
New Model Unions, 25-6
Nore Mutiny, 10
Northumberland Miners' Union, 30

O
Oldham lock-out, 23-4
Organisation for the Maintenance of Supplies (OMS), 70, 71
Osborne, Walter, 47
Osborne Judgement, 47
Owen, Robert, 17-8

P
Peel, Sir Robert, 13
Picketing, 29
Pitt, William, 9, *10*
Place, Francis, 13, *13*
Poland, 61
police strike (1919), 60, *60*
Prices and Incomes Act (1966), 84, 90
Prices and Incomes Board, 84

R
'Red Friday', 69
Reform Act (1867), 26
Rockingham, Marquis of, 6
Rowntree, Seerbohm, 41, 43

95

Royal Commissions
   children's employment in mines, 21
   trade unions (1867), 28-9
   coal industry (1919), 61-3
   Samuel Commission (1926), 69-70
   trade unions and employers associations (1966), 89-90
Russian Revolution (1917), 59, 60

S

Samuel, Sir Herbert, 69; Samuel Memorandum, 74
Sankey, Sir John, 61
Sawgrinders' Union, 28, 86
'scab', 11
Scottish Labour Party, 43
Seamen's Union, 51
Shaftesbury, Lord, 21
Shaw, George Bernard, 44
Shaw Tribunal, 77
shop stewards, 58, 80
Smith, Herbert, 70, *70*
Snowden, Philip, 68, 78
Syndicalists, 49

T

Taff Vale, 45, 48
Ten Hours Act (1847), 22
Thomas, J. H., 67, 70, 74, 78, *68*
Thorne, Will, 38
Tillet, Ben, 38-40, 44, 51, *54*
Tolpuddle, 19-21, 34, 51
Ton-y-Pandy, 50-1

Trades Disputes Act (1906), 46; (1927), 75
Trade Union Act (1871), 29
Trade Union Congress (TUC), 30-1, 55, 57, 78, 81, 85
   Economic Committee, 77
   General Council, 66-7, 69, 71, 74-5, 78, 82-4, 90
   General Secretary, 67, 68, 77
   Parliamentary Committee, 30-1, 44
Transport and General Workers Union (TGWU), 66, 77-8, 83, 86
Transport House, 78
Transport Workers' Federation (TWF), 50, 51, 54, 55
Triple Alliance, 55-6, 63, 66

V

Victoria, Queen, 42, 67

W

Warwickshire Agricultural Labourers Union, 34
Webb, Sidney and Beatrice, 44
Welfare State, 81, 82
Wells, H. G., 44
Whitley Councils, 60
Wilberforce, William, 7
Wilson, Harold, 84, 85
Woodcock, George, 83, 85, 89, *85*
World War, First, 57

Y

Young, Arthur, 7